Modern Critical Interpretations

William Faulkner's
Absalom, Absalom!

Modern Critical Interpretations

These and other titles in preparation

Modern Critical Interpretations

William Faulkner's
Absalom, Absalom!

Edited and with an introduction by
Harold Bloom
Sterling Professor of the Humanities
Yale University

Chelsea House Publishers ◇ *1987*
NEW YORK ◇ NEW HAVEN ◇ PHILADELPHIA

© 1987 by Chelsea House Publishers, a division
of Chelsea House Educational Communications, Inc.,
  95 Madison Avenue, New York, NY 10016
  345 Whitney Avenue, New Haven, CT 06511
  5014 West Chester Pike, Edgemont, PA 19028

Introduction © 1987 by Harold Bloom

Printed and bound in the United States of America

∞ The paper used in this publication meets the minimum
requirements of the American National Standard for
Permanence of Paper for Printed Library Materials,
Z39.48-1984.

Library of Congress Cataloging-in-Publication Data
William Faulkner's Absalom, Absalom!
  (Modern critical interpretations)
  Bibliography: p.
  Includes index.
  Summary: A collection of critical essays on Faulkner's novel
"Absalom, Absalom!" arranged in chronological order of
publication.
  1. Faulkner, William, 1897–1962. Absalom, Absalom!
[1. Faulkner, William, 1897–1962. Absalom, Absalom!
2. American literature—History and criticism] I. Bloom,
Harold. II. Series.
PS3511.A86A77   1987   813'.52   87-5210
ISBN 1-55546-039-9 (alk. paper)

Contents

Editor's Note

This book gathers together what I judge to be a representative selection of the best criticism available upon William Faulkner's novel *Absalom, Absalom!* I am grateful to John Rogers for his erudition in researching this volume. The critical essays are reprinted here in the chronological order of their original publication.

My introduction dissents from the general estimate that prefers *Absalom, Absalom!* to Faulkner's other major novels: *As I Lay Dying, The Sound and the Fury, Light in August.* John T. Irwin, precursor of what is now the prevalent mode of Faulknerian criticism, begins the chronological sequence with his psychoanalytically oriented study (heavily crossed by Nietzschean philosophy) of the patterns of incest and repetition in Faulkner's most ambitious novel. In the same mode, Gary Lee Stonum also investigates repetition and dispersal of the past in the present throughout *Absalom, Absalom!*

Carolyn Porter, centering upon Quentin's stance as narrator, situates the reader's dilemma in that stance: resisting the novel's obsessions puts one in the position of imitating Sutpen, the novel's obsessed protagonist. Faulkner's biographer, David Minter, contextualizes *Absalom, Absalom!* in Faulkner's own obsessions as to family and region.

In a Barthesian reading, Peter Brooks deftly analyzes many of the narrative perplexities of the novel. More historically, Eric J. Sundquist relates the guilt that pervades *Absalom, Absalom!* to the burden of the South's guilt. That guilt, extended to the nation, earlier and now, is the subject of James A. Snead in the volume's final essay. The "narrative erasure of blacks" in the novel is offered by Snead as another solution to *Absalom, Absalom!*'s puzzlements of form and meaning.

Introduction

No critic need invent William Faulkner's obsessions with what Nietzsche might have called the genealogy of the imagination. Recent critics of Faulkner, including David Minter, John T. Irwin, David M. Wyatt, and Richard H. King, have emphasized the novelist's profound need to believe himself to have been his own father in order to escape not only the Freudian family romance and literary anxieties of influence, but also the cultural dilemmas of what King terms "the Southern family romance." From *The Sound and the Fury* through the debacle of *A Fable,* Faulkner centers upon the sorrows of fathers and sons, to the disadvantage of mothers and daughters. No feminist critic ever will be happy with Faulkner. His brooding conviction that female sexuality is closely allied with death seems essential to all of his strongest fictions. It may even be that Faulkner's rhetorical economy, his wounded need to get his cosmos into a single sentence, is related to his fear that origin and end might prove to be one. Nietzsche prophetically had warned that origin and end were separate entities, and for the sake of life had to be kept apart, but Faulkner (strangely like Freud) seems to have known that the only Western trope participating neither in origin nor end is the image of the father.

By universal consent of critics and common readers, Faulkner now is recognized as the strongest American novelist of this century, clearly surpassing Hemingway and Fitzgerald, and standing as an equal in the sequence that includes Hawthorne, Melville, Mark Twain, and Henry James. Some critics might add Dreiser to this group; Faulkner himself curiously would have insisted upon Thomas Wolfe, a generous though dubious judgment. The American precursor for Faulkner was Sherwood Anderson, but perhaps only as an impetus; the true American forerunner is the poetry of T. S. Eliot, as Judith L. Sensibar demonstrates. But the truer precursor for Faulkner's fiction is Conrad, inescapable for the American novelists of Faulkner's generation, including Hemingway and Fitzgerald. Comparison to Conrad is dangerous for any novelist, and clearly Faulkner did not achieve a *Nostromo*. But his work of the decade 1929–39 does include four permanent books: *The Sound and the Fury, As I Lay Dying, Light in August,* and *Absalom, Absalom!* If one adds *Sanctuary* and *The Wild Palms,* and *The Hamlet* and *Go Down, Moses* in the early forties, then the combined effect is extraordinary.

From Malcolm Cowley on, critics have explained this effect as the consequence of the force of mythmaking, at once personal and local. Cleanth Brooks, the rugged final champion of the New Criticism, essentially reads Faulkner as he does Eliot's *The Waste Land,* finding the hidden God of the normative Christian tradition to be the basis for Faulkner's attitude towards nature. Since Brooks calls Faulkner's stance Wordsworthian, and finds Wordsworthian nature a Christian vision also, the judgment involved necessarily has its problematical elements. Walter Pater, a critic in a very different tradition, portrayed a very different Wordsworth in terms that seem to me not inapplicable to Faulkner:

> Religious sentiment, consecrating the affections and natural regrets of the human heart, above all, that pitiful awe and care for the perishing human clay, of which relic-worship is but the corruption, has always had much to do with localities, with the thoughts which attach themselves to actual scenes and places. Now what is true of it everywhere, is truest of it in those secluded valleys where one generation after another maintains the same abiding place; and it was on this side, that Wordsworth apprehended religion most strongly. Consisting, as it did so much, in the recognition of local sanctities, in the habit of connecting the stones and trees of a particular spot of earth with the great events of life, till the low walls, the green mounds, the half-obliterated epitaphs seemed full of voices, and a sort of natural oracles, the very religion of those people of the dales, appeared but as another link between them and the earth, and was literally a religion of nature.

A kind of stoic natural religion pervades this description, something close to the implicit faith of old Isaac McCaslin in *Go Down, Moses.* It seems unhelpful to speak of "residual Christianity" in Faulkner, as Cleanth Brooks does. Hemingway and Fitzgerald, in their nostalgias, perhaps were closer to a Christian ethos than Faulkner was in his great phase. Against current critical judgment, I prefer *As I Lay Dying* and *Light in August* to *The Sound and the Fury* and *Absalom, Absalom!*, partly because the first two are more primordial in their vision, closer to the stoic intensities of their author's kind of natural piety. There is an *otherness* in Lena Grove and the Bundrens that would have moved Wordsworth, that is, the Wordsworth of *The Tale of Margaret, Michael,* and *The Old Cumberland Beggar.* A curious movement that is also a stasis becomes Faulkner's pervasive trope for Lena. Though he invokes the imagery of Keats's urn, Faulkner seems to have had the harvest-girl of Keats's *To Autumn* more in mind, or even the stately figures of the *Ode to Indolence.* We remember Lena Grove as stately, calm, a person yet a process, a serene and patient consciousness, full of wonder, too much a unitary being to need even her author's variety of stoic courage.

The uncanniness of this representation is exceeded by the Bundrens, whose plangency testifies to Faulkner's finest rhetorical achievement. *As I Lay Dying* may be the most original novel ever written by an American. Obviously it is not free of the deepest influence Faulkner knew as a novelist. The language is never Conradian, and yet the sense of the reality principle is. But there is nothing in Conrad like Darl Bundren, not even in *The Secret Agent. As I Lay Dying* is Faulkner's strongest protest against the facticity of literary convention, against the force of the familial past, which tropes itself in fiction as the repetitive form of narrative imitating prior narrative. The book is a sustained nightmare, insofar as it is Darl's book, which is to say, Faulkner's book, or the book of his daemon.

II

Canonization is a process of enshrining creative misinterpretations, and no one need lament this. Still, one element that ensues from this process all too frequently is the not very creative misinterpretation in which the idiosyncratic is distorted into the normative. Churchwardenly critics who assimilate the Faulkner of the thirties to spiritual, social, and moral ortho-doxy can and do assert Faulkner himself as their preceptor. But this is the Faulkner of the fifties, Nobel laureate, State Department envoy and author of *A Fable,* a book of a badness simply astonishing for Faulkner. The best of the normative critics, Cleanth Brooks, reads even *As I Lay Dying* as a quest for community, an exaltation of the family, an affirmation of Christian values. The Bundrens manifestly constitute one of the most terrifying visions of the family romance in the history of literature. But their extrem-ism is not eccentric in the 1929–39 world of Faulkner's fiction. That world is founded upon a horror of families, a limbo of outcasts, an evasion of all values other than stoic endurance. It is a world in which what is silent in the other Bundrens speaks in Darl, what is veiled in the Compsons is uncovered in Quentin. So tangled are these returns of the repressed with what continues to be estranged that phrases like "the violation of the natural" and "the denial of the human" become quite meaningless when applied to Faulkner's greater fictions. In that world, the natural is itself a violation and the human already a denial. Is the weird quest of the Bundrens a violation of the natural, or is it what Blake would have called a terrible triumph for the selfish virtues of the natural heart? Darl judges it to be the latter, but Darl luminously denies the sufficiency of the human, at the cost of what seems schizophrenia.

Marxist criticism of imaginative literature, if it had not regressed abominably in our country so that now it is a travesty of the dialectical suppleness of Adorno and Benjamin, would find a proper subject in the difficult relationship between the 1929 business panic and *As I Lay Dying*. Perhaps the self-destruction of our delusive political economy helped free Faulkner from whatever inhibitions, communal and personal, had kept him earlier from a saga like that of the Bundrens. Only an authentic seer can give permanent form to a prophecy like *As I Lay Dying,* which puts severely into question every received notion we have of the natural and the human. Darl asserts he has no mother, while taunting his enemy brother, Jewel, with the insistence that Jewel's mother was a horse. Their little brother, Vardaman, says, "My mother is a fish." The mother, dead and undead, is uncannier even than these children when she confesses the truth of her existence, her rejecting vision of her children:

> I could just remember how my father used to say that the reason for living was to get ready to stay dead a long time. And when I would have to look at them day after day, each with his and her single and selfish thought, and blood strange to each other blood and strange to mine, and think that this seemed to be the only way I could get ready to stay dead, I would hate my father for having ever planted me. I would look forward to the times when they faulted, so I could whip them. When the switch fell I could feel it upon my flesh; when it welted and ridged it was my blood that ran, and I would think with each blow of the switch: Now you are aware of me! Now I am something in your secret and selfish life, who have marked your blood with my own for ever and ever.

This veritable apocalypse of any sense of otherness is no mere "denial of community." Nor are the Bundrens any "mimesis of essential nature." They are a super-mimesis, an over-representation mocking nature while shadowing it. What matters in major Faulkner is that the people have gone back, not to nature but to some abyss before the Creation-Fall. Eliot insisted that Joyce's imagination was eminently orthodox. This can be doubted, but in Faulkner's case there is little sense in baptizing his imagination. One sees why he preferred reading the Old Testament to the New, remarking that the former was stories and the latter, ideas. The remark is inadequate except insofar as it opposes Hebraic to Hellenistic representation of character. There is little that is Homeric about the Bundrens, or Sophoclean about the Compsons. Faulkner's irony is neither classical nor romantic, neither Greek nor German. It does not say one thing while meaning another nor trade in contrasts between expectation and fulfillment. Instead, it juxtaposes incommensurable realities: of self and other, of parent and child, of past and future. When Gide maintained that Faulkner's people lacked souls, he simply failed to observe that Faulkner's ironies were biblical. To which an amendment must be added. In Faulkner, only the ironies are biblical. What Faulkner's people lack is the blessing; they cannot contend for a time without boundaries. Yahweh will make no covenant with them. Their agon therefore is neither the Greek one for the foremost place nor the Hebrew one for the blessing, which honors the father and the mother. Their agon is the hopeless one of waiting for their doom to lift.

III

In a cosmos where only the ironies are biblical, the self, like the father and the past, becomes what Nietzsche called a "numinous shadow," an ancestor rather than a personal possession. Where the self is so estranged, we are not on Shakespeare's stage but on John Webster's, so that the Thomas Sutpen of *Absalom, Absalom!* is in some respects another Jacobean hero-villain who would end by saying (if he could), "I limned this night-piece, and it was my best." *Absalom, Absalom!* is a tragic farce, like *The White Devil,* and shares in some of the formal difficulties that are endemic in tragic farce. Rather than add to the distinguished discourse on the narrative perplexities that figure so richly in *Absalom, Absalom!,* I wish to address the question of comparative value. Does the novel have the aesthetic dignity that justifies its problematic form, or have we canonized it prematurely?

For reasons that I do not altogether comprehend, *Absalom, Absalom!* seems to me a less original book than the three great novels by Faulkner that preceded it: *The Sound and the Fury, As I Lay Dying, Light in August.*

The precursors—Conrad profoundly, Joyce, Eliot, and even Tennyson more superficially—manifest themselves in Faulkner's text more overtly than they do in the three earlier works. One misses also the intensely sympathetic figures—Dilsey, Darl Bundren, Lena Grove—and their dreadful obverses—Jason Compson, Addie Bundren, Percy Grimm—who help make the three earlier masterpieces so memorable. A shadow falls upon Faulkner's originality, both of style and of representation, in *Absalom, Absalom!* Can that shadow be named?

There seems to be an element of obscurantism in *Absalom, Absalom!*, even as there is in Conrad's *Heart of Darkness*. I do not find any obscurantism in *As I Lay Dying* or *Light in August*, even as *Nostromo* and *Victory* seem to be free of it. It hovers uneasily in *The Sound and the Fury* as it does in *Lord Jim*, yet it scarcely mars those books. Sometimes in *Absalom*, as in *Heart of Darkness*, I lose confidence that the author knows precisely what he is talking about. The consequence is a certain bathos which necessarily diminishes the aesthetic dignity of the work:

> " 'You see, I had a design in my mind. Whether it was a good or a bad design is beside the point; the question is, Where did I make the mistake in it, what did I do or misdo in it, whom or what injure by it to the extent which this would indicate. I had a design. To accomplish it I should require money, a house, a plantation, slaves, a family—incidentally of course, a wife. I set out to acquire these, asking no favor of any man. I even risked my life at one time, as I told you, though as I also told you I did not undertake this risk purely and simply to gain a wife, though it did have that result. But that is beside the point also: suffice that I had the wife, accepted her in good faith, with no reservations about myself, and I expected as much from them. I did not even demand, mind, as one of my obscure origin might have been expected to do (or at least be condoned in the doing) out of ignorance of gentility in dealing with gentleborn people. I did not demand; I accepted them at their own valuation while insisting on my own part upon explaining fully about myself and my progenitors: yet they deliberately withheld from me the one fact which I have reason to know they were aware would have caused me to decline the entire matter, otherwise they would not have withheld it from me—a fact which I did not learn until after my son was born. And even then I did not act hastily. I could have reminded them of these wasted years, these

years which would now leave me behind with my schedule not only the amount of elapsed time which their number represented, but that compensatory amount of time represented by their number which I should now have to spend to advance myself once more to the point I had reached and lost. But I did not. I merely explained how this new fact rendered it impossible that this woman and child be incorporated in my design, and following which, as I told you, I made no attempt to keep not only that which I might consider myself to have earned at the risk of my life but which had been given to me by signed testimonials, but on the contrary I declined and resigned all right and claim to this in order that I might repair whatever injustice I might be considered to have done by so providing for the two persons whom I might be considered to have deprived of anything I might later possess: and this was agreed to, mind; agreed to between the two parties. And yet, and after more than thirty years, more than thirty years after my conscience had finally assured me that if I had done an injustice, I had done what I could to rectify it——' and Grandfather not saying 'Wait' now but saying, hollering maybe even: 'Conscience? Conscience? Good God, man, what else did you expect? Didn't the very affinity and instinct for misfortune of a man who had spent that much time in a monastery even, let alone one who had lived that many years as you lived them, tell you better than that? didn't the dread and fear of females which you must have drawn in with the primary mammalian milk teach you better? What kind of abysmal and purblind innocence could that have been which someone told you to call virginity? what conscience to trade with which would have warranted you in the belief that you could have bought immunity from her for no other coin but justice?'——"

This is Sutpen, as reported by Quentin's Grandfather, and ends with the latter admonishing Sutpen. For the rhetoric here of both men not to seem excessive, Sutpen must be of some eminence and his "design" of some consequence. But nothing in the novel persuades one of Sutpen's stature or of his design's meaningfulness. Like Kurtz in *Heart of Darkness*, Sutpen is a blind will in a cognitive vacuum; both figures seem to represent nothing more than a Nietzschean spirit of mere resentment, rather than the will's deep revenge against time, and time's "It was." Faulkner evidently was persuaded of Sutpen's importance, if only as a vital synecdoche for southern history. More a process than a man, Sutpen has drive without personality. One can remember a few of his acts, but none of his words, let alone his thoughts—if he has thoughts. He is simply too abrupt a mythic representation, rather than a man who becomes a myth. Only the scope of his failure interests Faulkner, rather than anything he is or means as a person.

Good critics confronting *Absalom, Absalom!* are fascinated by its intricate and enormous narrative procedures and by its genealogical patterns: doubling, incest, repetition, revenge—as John Irwin catalogs them. But narrative complications and structures of human desire, however titanic, are not necessarily aesthetic achievements. The Johnsonian questions, decisive for the common reader, always remain: how significant is the action that is represented, and how persuasive is the representation of the actors? Abstractly, the founding of a house and clan ought to outweigh the lunatic quest to bury a bad mother in the face of appalling obstacles, and yet Faulkner fails to make the former project as vital as the latter. Sutpen's design does not in itself move me, while the Bundrens' journey never loses its capacity to shock me into a negative Sublime. As a minority of one (so far as I can tell), I would yield to other critics on the greatness of *Absalom, Absalom!*, except that the best of them simply assume the eminence and mythic splendor of the book.

Time may reveal such assumptions to be accurate and thus justify readings that take delight in aspects of the book that make it more problematic than nearly any other comparable novel. Still, Faulkner's *A Fable*, surely his worst book by any critical standards, will sustain post-Structuralist readings almost as well as *Absalom, Absalom!* does. Perhaps Faulkner's most comprehensive and ambitious novel justifies its vast inclusiveness that is so uneasily allied to its deliberately unfinished quality. But Sutpen is indeed more like Conrad's Kurtz than like Melville's Ahab, in that his obsessions are not sufficiently metaphysical. Sutpen's Hundred is too much Kurtz's Africa, and too little the whiteness of the whale.

Doubling and Incest / Repetition and Revenge

John T. Irwin

> *But he wouldn't want his sister to marry one.*

The epigraph to this essay is a reference to the racial slur that goes, "I don't have anything against Negroes, but I wouldn't want my sister to marry one." Its implied argument is that integration leads to miscegenation, and that miscegenation is a threat to the purity of white women and an affront to the manhood of their protectors—their fathers and brothers. In Faulkner's *Absalom, Absalom!* Henry Sutpen kills his half brother Charles Bon, who is part black, to prevent Bon from marrying their sister Judith. At one point in the narrative Bon, in a mixture of despair and grief at his father's refusal to acknowledge him as his son, replies to Henry's declaration "*You are my brother*" with the taunt "*No I'm not. I'm the nigger that's going to sleep with your sister. Unless you stop me, Henry.*" In the story of the Sutpens the threat of miscegenation between Bon and Judith is also a threat of brother-sister incest, and it is another brother, Henry, who acts to stop these threats. This archetype of the brother who must kill to protect or avenge the honor of his sister pervades *Absalom, Absalom!* It occurs, first of all, in the very title of the novel. In the Old Testament (2 Sam. 13), Absalom, one of David's sons, kills his brother Amnon for raping their sister Tamar. The archetype presents itself again in Quentin Compson, the principal narrator of *Absalom.* From *The Sound and the Fury* we know that Quentin is in love with his own sister Candace and that he is tormented by his inability to

From *Doubling and Incest / Repetition and Revenge: A Speculative Reading of Faulkner.*
© 1975 by the Johns Hopkins University Press.

play the role of the avenging brother and kill her seducer. Of the many levels of meaning in *Absalom,* the deepest level is to be found in the symbolic identification of incest and miscegenation and in the relationship of this symbolic identification both to Quentin Compson's personal history in *The Sound and the Fury* and to the story that Quentin narrates in *Absalom, Absalom!*

There are, of course, four narrators in the novel—Quentin, his father, his roommate Shreve, and Miss Rosa Coldfield—but of these four certainly Quentin is the central narrator, not just because he ends up knowing more of the story than do the other three, but because the other three only function as narrators in relation to Quentin. When Mr. Compson or Shreve or Miss Rosa Coldfield tell what they know or conjecture of the Sutpen's story, they are talking, either actually or imaginatively, to Quentin. One reason that the voices of the different narrators sound so much alike is that we hear those voices filtered through the mind of a single listener: Quentin's consciousness is the fixed point of view from which the reader *overhears* the various narrators, Quentin included. Since Quentin is the principal narrative consciousness in *Absalom,* and since the story of the Sutpens contains numerous gaps that must be filled by conjecture on the part of the narrators, it is not surprising that the narrative bears a striking resemblance to Quentin's own personal history and that of his family. Quentin uses his own experience of family life in a small Southern town to try to understand the motives for events in the story of Thomas Sutpen and his children, particularly that central enigmatic event to which the narration continually returns—the murder of Charles Bon by his best friend, Henry Sutpen. This is not to imply that the factual similarities between the stories of the Sutpen and Compson families are a product of Quentin's imagination, but to point out that, given these similarities of fact, Quentin as creative narrator could easily presume similarity of motivation. It is a mutual process in which what Quentin knows of the motivations in his own family life illuminates the story of the Sutpens and, in turn, the events in the Sutpens' story help Quentin to understand his own experiences.

That the story Quentin narrates resembles his own story has been noted by critics, but they have considered this parallel to be of secondary importance. Richard Poirier says that Quentin may see in the murder of Charles Bon "a distorted image of his own failure in *The Sound and the Fury* to defend the honor of his sister, Caddy, and of the incest which he claims to have committed. . . . But it is well to remember that Quentin's interest in Sutpen's story transcends any reference he finds in it for such personal problems, which, after all, we are acquainted with only from observing his activity outside the context of *Absalom, Absalom!* Had Quentin assumed the luxury of treating the Sutpen story merely as an objectification of some personal obsession, the total effect of the novel would have partaken of the overindulgent and romantic self-dramatization of Rosa's soliloquy" (" 'Strange Gods' in Jefferson, Mississippi: Analysis of *Absalom, Absalom!*"). Poirier's assumption that Quentin's personal history, because it is contained in another novel, is therefore inapplicable to *Absalom* seems to be a particularly inappropriate principle to apply to the works of a writer like Faulkner, whose novels are parts of a single continuing story. Faulkner did not need to make Quentin Compson a narrator of *Absalom,* nor did he need to involve the Compson family in the story of the Sutpens. The fact that he did both indicates that what we know of Quentin Compson and his family from *The Sound and the Fury* is somehow material to the meaning of Sutpen's story. When Faulkner, in one of the conferences he gave at the University of Virginia, was asked whether the central character in *Absalom* was Sutpen or Quentin, he replied that Sutpen was the central figure but that the novel was "incidentally the story of Quentin Compson's hatred of the bad qualities in the country he loves." And on another occasion, in commenting on the relationship of Quentin's personal history to the story of the Sutpens, Faulkner remarked that "every time any character gets into a book no matter how minor, he's actually telling his biography—that's all anyone ever does, he tells his own biography, talking about himself, in a thousand different terms, but himself. Quentin was still trying to get God to tell him why, in *Absalom, Absalom!* as he was in *The Sound and the Fury.*" Poirier's contention that Quentin's narrative act is an attempt to avoid merely objectifying a personal obsession, an attempt to avoid becoming like Rosa Coldfield in her narration, ignores the fact that for Quentin the objectification of subjective contents is an effort to give a personal obsession a more than personal significance.

To what extent, then, does the story that Quentin tells in *Absalom* resemble his own life story in *The Sound and the Fury?* We noted first of all that Quentin's failure to kill Candace's seducer and thus fulfill the role of protective brother has its reverse image in Henry's murder of Bon to safeguard the honor of their sister. Also, Quentin's incestuous love for Candace is mirrored by Bon's love for Judith. That Quentin identifies with both Henry, the brother as protector, and Bon, the brother as seducer, is not extraordinary, for in Quentin's narrative they are not so much two separate figures as two aspects of the same figure. Quentin projects onto the characters of Bon and Henry opposing elements in his own personality—Bon represents Quentin's unconsciously motivated desire for his sister Candace, while Henry represents the conscious repression or punishment of that desire. This separation of the unacceptable elements from the acceptable elements in the self, this splitting of Quentin's personality into a bad half and a good half, with the subsequent tormenting of the good half by the bad and the punishment of the bad half by the good, involves a kind of narrative bipolarity typical of both compulsion neurosis and schizophrenia. The split is the result of the self's inability to handle ambivalence, in this case, Quentin's failure to reconcile his simultaneous attraction to and repulsion by the incestuous desire for his sister. The solution is primitive and effective: one simply splits the good-bad self into two separate people. Indeed, at the very beginning of the novel when he first visits Miss Rosa, Quentin is presented as a divided self: "he would listen to two separate Quentins now—the Quentin Compson preparing for Harvard in the South, the deep South dead since 1865 and peopled with garrulous outraged baffled ghosts, listening, having to listen, to one of the ghosts which had refused to lie still even longer than most had, telling him about old ghost-times; and the Quentin Compson who was still too young to deserve yet to be a ghost, but nevertheless having to be one for all that, since he was born and bred in the deep South the same as she was—two separate Quentins now talking to one another in the long silence of notpeople, in notlanguage." If at points during the narrative Quentin divides his personality between the characters of Bon and Henry, at other points Henry and Bon merge into one figure by exchanging roles. For example, though Henry ends up as the avenging brother, yet, as Mr. Compson says, "it must have been Henry who seduced Judith, not Bon: seduced her along with himself." And though Bon dies playing the role of the dark seducer, yet he offers to give up Judith and never trouble the Sutpens again if his father will only acknowledge his existence. When Sutpen ignores him, Bon's deliberate provoking of Henry amounts almost to a suicidal self-punishment.

Clearly, the relationship between Henry and Bon is a form of doubling: the hero-worshiping Henry imitates Bon's manners, speech, and dress, while Bon (as Shreve conjectures) looks at Henry and thinks "not *there but for the intervening leaven of that blood which we do not have in common is my skull, my brow, sockets, shape and angle of jaw and chin and some of my thinking behind it, and which he could see in my face in his turn if he but knew to look as I know* but *there, just behind a little, obscured a little by that alien blood whose admixing was necessary in order that he exist is the face of the man who shaped us both out of that blind chancy darkness which we call the future; there—there— at any moment, second, I shall penetrate by something of will and intensity and dreadful need, and strip that alien leavening from it and look not on my brother's face whom I did not know I possessed and hence never missed, but my father's, out of the shadow of whose absence my spirit's posthumeity has never escaped.*" On another occasion Bon, debating this family resemblance with himself, divides into two voices that reflect Quentin's own splitting: "one part of him said *He has my brow my skull my jaw my hands* and the other said *Wait. Wait. You cant know yet. You cannot know yet whether what you see is what you are looking at or what you are believing.*" That last remark is an apt description as well of Quentin's relationship to the story of Charles Bon, for it is impossible for us to tell whether many of the things that Quentin says about Bon are what he knows or what he simply believes.

In the doubling between Bon and Henry, Bon plays the role of the shadow—the dark self that is made to bear the consciously unacceptable desires repudiated by the bright half of the mind. Throughout the novel, Bon is identified with the image of the shadow. Mr. Compson speaks of Bon's "impenetrable and shadowy character. Yes, shadowy: a myth, a phantom: something which they engendered and created whole themselves; some effluvium of Sutpen blood and character, as though as a man he did not exist at all." Miss Rosa calls Bon "a shadow with a name." And she says that "he had left no more trace" in her sister's house than if "he had been but a shape, a shadow." At one point, Quentin and Shreve's reconstruction of Bon's character is described as "the creating of this shade whom they discussed (rather, existed in)." The contrast between Bon's role as the dark self and Henry's as the bright self is made particularly clear in Bon's imagined appraisal of his younger brother: "*this flesh and bone and spirit which stemmed from the same source that mine did, but which sprang in quiet peace and contentment and ran in steady even though monotonous sunlight, where that which he bequeathed me sprang in hatred and outrage and unforgiving and ran in shadow.*" Realizing that Quentin projects his own unacceptable impulses onto Bon as the shadow self, we understand the deeper significance of the imagery that Quentin employs in imagining the final confrontation between the brothers. Bon and Henry ride up to the house, one falls behind or one draws ahead, they face each other and speak, "*Dont you pass the shadow of this post, this branch, Charles; and I am going to pass it, Henry.*" And when Quentin unwillingly accompanies Rosa Coldfield out to the Sutpen place to discover the secret of the old dark house, he approaches the rotting gate posts and looks apprehensively about, "wondering what had cast the shadow which Bon was not to pass alive" and "wishing that Henry were there now to stop Miss Coldfield and turn them back."

Bon serves as the shadow self of Quentin by acting within Quentin's narrative as the shadow self of Henry. That Henry vicariously satisfies his own desire for his sister Judith by identifying himself with her lover is first suggested by Mr. Compson. He says that Henry pleaded his friend's suit better than Bon could himself, "as though it actually were the brother who had put the spell on the sister, seduced her to his own vicarious image which walked and breathed with Bon's body." And he comments, "perhaps this is the pure and perfect incest: the brother realizing that the sister's virginity must be destroyed in order to have existed at all, taking that virginity in the person of the brother-in-law, the man whom he would be if he could become, metamorphose into, the lover, the husband; by whom he would be despoiled, choose for despoiler, if he could become, metamorphose into the sister, the mistress, the bride. Perhaps that is what went on, not in Henry's mind but in his soul." Clearly, the relationship between Henry and Bon is ambivalent—that characteristic love/hate between the bright and the dark selves. Mr. Compson says that Henry loved Bon and that Bon "not only loved Judith after his fashion but he loved Henry too and . . . in a deeper sense than merely after his fashion. Perhaps in his fatalism he loved Henry the better of the two." Indeed, Mr. Compson suggests that Bon's marriage to Judith would have represented a vicarious consummation of the love between Bon and Henry. Yet between the two there is a veiled antagonism as well. Bon's dark Latin sensibility is galled by Henry's clodhopper Puritanism. When Bon and Henry are in New Orleans, Bon gradually reveals the existence of his octoroon mistress to prevent Henry, with his shocked provincial morality, from challenging him to a duel, for, as Bon sardonically remarks, he would have to give Henry the choice of weapons and he would prefer not to fight with axes. And later, in an imagined conversation, Henry tells Bon, "I used to think that I would hate the man that I would have to look at every day and whose every move and action and speech would say to me, I have seen and touched parts of your sister's body that you will never see and touch: and now I know that I shall hate him and that's why I want that man to be you."

As Otto Rank has pointed out in his classic study of doubling, the brother and the shadow are two of the most common forms that the figure of the double assumes. Rank locates the origin of doubling in narcissism, specifically in that guilt which the narcissistic ego feels at "the distance between the ego-ideal and the attained reality" (*The Double*). In this case the ego's towering self-love and consequent overestimation of its own worth lead to the guilty rejection of all instincts and desires that don't fit its ideal image of itself. The rejected instincts and desires are cast out of the self, repressed internally only to return externally personified in the double, where they can be at once vicariously satisfied and punished. The double evokes the ego's love because it is a copy of the ego, but it evokes the ego's fear and hatred as well because it is a copy with a difference. It is this element of sameness with a difference that gives the figure of the double that quality of the uncanny which we will discuss later in relation to the repetitive structure of doubling. The difference that the ego senses in the double is the implicit presence of the unconscious and particularly that form of unconsciousness which the narcissistic ego finds most offensive to its self-esteem—death. In the myth, Narcissus sees his image reflected in the water; he recognizes the image as himself, yet sees that it is shadowed on a medium whose fluidity, whose lack of differentiation, whose anarchy continually threaten to dissolve the unity of that image at the very moment that the medium itself seems to supply the force to sustain that image. What Narcissus sees is that unified image of his conscious life buoyed up from moment to moment by a medium whose very constitution, in relation to the ego, seems, paradoxically, to be dissolution and death. Rank points out that in myth and literature the appearance of the double is often a harbinger of death and that just as often the ego attempts to protect itself by killing the double, only to find that this is "really a suicidal act." It is in the mechanism of narcissistic self-love that Rank finds the explanation for that "denouement of madness, almost regularly leading to suicide, which is so frequently linked with pursuit by the double." In this mechanism, the ego does not so much fear death as find unbearable "the *expectation* of the unavoidable destiny of death." Rank quotes Wilde's Dorian Gray: "I have no terror of Death. It is only the *coming* of Death that terrifies me." Or as Poe's Roderick Usher says, "In this unnerved—in this pitiable condition—I feel that the period will sooner or later arrive when I must abandon life and reason together, in some struggle with the grim phantasm, Fear." Roderick is driven mad by the image of his own fate which he sees in the progressive physical dissolution of his twin sister Madeline, and he is literally frightened to death when Madeline, whom he has prematurely buried in an unconscious attempt at self-defense, returns from the tomb as a figure of death-in-life. The narrator succinctly remarks that Roderick fell "a victim to the terrors he had anticipated." Rank notes that "the normally unconscious thought of the approaching destruction of the self—the most general example of the repression of an unendurable certainty—torments these unfortunates with the conscious idea of their eternal inability to return, an idea from which release is only possible in death. Thus we have the strange paradox of the suicide who voluntarily seeks death in order to free himself of the intolerable thanatophobia." There is as well about the suicidal murder of the double a suggestion of the *liebestod,* as if the only way that the ego could be joined with the beloved yet fearful other self is by a reflexive death in which the ego plunges itself into the otherness of the unconscious evoked by the double.

Both the narcissistic origin of doubling and the scenario of madness leading to the suicidal murder of the double help to illuminate the internal narrative of Quentin Compson's last day given in *The Sound and the Fury* and in turn to illuminate the story he tells in *Absalom*. In the fictive time of the novels, Quentin and Shreve's joint narration, which occupies the last half of *Absalom,* takes place in January 1910, and Quentin's suicide occurs six months later on June 2, 1910, but the account of that suicide is given in a novel that appeared seven years before *Absalom*. Since we already know Quentin's end when we observe his attempt in *Absalom* to explain the reason for Bon's murder, we not only participate in that effort but also engage at the same time in an analogous effort of our own to explain Quentin's murder of himself. And it is only when we see in the murder of Bon by Henry what Quentin saw in it—that Quentin's own situation appears to be a repetition of the earlier story—that we begin to understand the reason for Quentin's suicide. And this whole repetitive structure is made even more problematic by the fact that the explanation which Quentin gives for Bon's murder (that Bon is black, i.e., the shadow self) may well be simply the return of the repressed—simply an unconscious projection of Quentin's own psychic history. Quentin's situation becomes endlessly repetitive insofar as he constantly creates the predecessors of that situation in his narration of past events. And to escape from that kind of repetition, one must escape from the self. . . .

In the story of the Sutpens, Quentin also finds a reenactment of the way that the fate of a father is passed on to a son. When Sutpen was a child, he received an affront from the black servant of a rich plantation owner. He was told that he could not come to the front door of the planter's house, he had to go around to the back because he was white trash, because he and his family were not as good as the plantation owner. Comparing the plantation owner with his own father, Sutpen rejects his father as a model and adopts the plantation owner as his surrogate father, as his model for what a man should be. And Sutpen feels the same ambivalence toward him that a son would feel for a father. At first, he considers killing him, but then he realizes that he doesn't want to do away with the plantation owner, he wants to become the plantation owner. The ruthless odyssey on which Sutpen embarks is a quest for revenge for the affront that he suffered as a boy—not revenge against a system in which the rich and powerful can affront the poor and powerless but against the luck of birth that made him one of the poor when he should have been one of the rich. Like Gatsby, Sutpen distinguishes between the "Platonic" and the "merely personal." Ideally, he accepts the justice of that mastery which the powerful have over the powerless, which the rich planter has over the poor boy, a father over his son. The fact that circumstance happened to start Sutpen off by casting him in the role of the powerless, poor boy is merely personal. A mere stroke of chance does not invalidate that hierarchy—or rather, patriarchy—of power. Sutpen seeks revenge within the rules of patriarchal power for the affront that he suffered; he does not try to show the injustice of the system, but rather to show that he is as good as any man in the system. If the planter is powerful because he is rich, then Sutpen will have his revenge by becoming richer and more powerful than the planter. And he will pass that wealth and power on to his son, doing for his son what his own father could not do for him. Sutpen comes to terms with the traumatic affront that he suffered as a boy by accepting the impersonal justice of it even though he feels its personal inappropriateness. He incorporates into himself the patriarchal ideal from which that affront sprang in much the same way that a son comes to terms with the image of his father as a figure of mastery and power by impersonalizing and internalizing that image as the superego, accepting the justice of the father's mastery even though that mastery has been exercised against the son. It is a mechanism by which the son tries to overcome the mastery of the personal father while maintaining the mastery of fatherhood—a mechanism in which the personal father dies without the son's having to kill him. Accepting this ideal of patriarchal power, Sutpen determines his fate—to repeat periodically that traumatic affront but in a different role. Henceforth, he will no longer receive the affront, he will deliver it. Thus, he rejects his first wife and son because they are not good enough to share the position to which he aspires. And he passes that fated repetition on to his sons—to Charles Bon, who returns thirty years later seeking admittance to the rich plantation owner's "house" (and thereby represents the return of that repressed traumatic affront of Sutpen's boyhood) and to Henry, who, acting as his father's surrogate, delivers the final affront to Bon, killing him at the gates of the house to prevent his entering.

In his interviews at the University of Virginia, Faulkner repeatedly pointed out that *Absalom* is a revenge story—indeed, a double revenge story: Sutpen's revenge for the affront that he suffered as a boy and Bon's revenge for the affront that he and his mother suffered at Sutpen's hands during Sutpen's quest for revenge. Faulkner said of Sutpen: "He wanted revenge as he saw it, but also he wanted to establish the fact that man is immortal, that man, if he is man, cannot be inferior to another man through artificial standards or circumstances. What he was trying to do—when he was a boy, he had gone to the front door of a big house and somebody, a servant, said, Go around to the back door. He said, I'm going to be the one that lives in the big house, I'm going to establish a dynasty, I don't care how, and he violated all the rules of decency and honor and pity and compassion, and the fates took revenge on him." Sutpen wants revenge not against the injustice of that mastery which the powerful have over the powerless, but against those "artificial standards or circumstances" that determine who are the powerful and who the powerless, against the artificial standard of inherited wealth and the circumstances of one's birth. Faulkner says that Sutpen in his quest for revenge violated all the rules of decency and honor and pity and compassion. But there is one rule that Sutpen does not violate, and that is the rule of power. For the rule that Sutpen follows is that real power springs not from the external, artificial advantages of birth and inherited wealth but from something internal: for Sutpen the source of real power is the force of the individual will. In any group of men, power belongs to the man whose will is strong enough to seize that power and hold it against his fellow men. But that brings us face to face with the central paradox of Sutpen's quest—that he seeks revenge on the artificial standards of birth and inherited wealth as the determinants of power by setting out to establish a dynasty—that is, by trying to confer those very same artificial advantages on his son. Faulkner gives us the key to this paradox when he says that Sutpen "wanted revenge as he saw it, but also he wanted to establish the fact that man is immortal, that man, if he is man, cannot be inferior to another man through artificial standards or circumstances." It is a puzzling statement. First of all, what does it mean to equate Sutpen's attempt to establish that man is immortal with his effort to prove that one man cannot be inferior to another through artificial standards or circumstances? And then, what does it mean to link these two with the quest for revenge?

The idea that lies behind Faulkner's statement is what Nietzsche called "the revenge against time." To understand what this idea involves, let us compare for a moment the careers of Jay Gatsby and Thomas Sutpen. Clearly, what Gatsby and Sutpen both seek in their quests is to alter the past—to repeat the past and correct it. As Sutpen in the role of the poor boy suffered an affront from the rich plantation owner, so Gatsby as the poor boy was rejected by the rich girl Daisy Buchanan, and as the former affront initiated Sutpen's grand design to get land, build a mansion, and establish a dynasty, that is, to repeat the past situation but with Sutpen now in the role of the affronter rather than the affronted and to pass on to his son the rich man's power to affront the poor and powerless, so Daisy's rejection of Gatsby initiates Gatsby's dream of acquiring a fortune, owning a great house, and winning Daisy back, his dream of repeating the past by marrying Daisy this time and obliterating everything that occurred between that rejection and his winning her back. When Nick Carraway realizes the enormity of Gatsby's dream, he tells him, "You can't repeat the past," and Gatsby with his Sutpen-like innocence replies, "Why of course you can." As Sutpen rejected his powerless, real father as a model in favor of the powerful plantation owner, so Gatsby rejected his father who was a failure, changed his name from Gatz to Gatsby, and adopted the self-made man Dan Cody as his surrogate father. But now the question arises, Why does the attempt to repeat the past and correct it turn into the revenge against time? Nietzsche's answer is worth quoting at length:

> "To redeem those who lived in the past and to recreate all 'it was' into a 'thus I willed it'—that alone should I call redemption. Will—that is the name of the liberator and joy-bringer; thus I taught you, my friends. But now learn this too: the will itself is still a prisoner. Willing liberates; but what is it that puts even the liberator himself in fetters? 'It was'—that is the name of the will's gnashing of teeth and most secret melancholy. Powerless against what has been done, he is an angry spectator of all that is past. The will cannot will backwards; and that he cannot break time and time's covetousness, that is the will's loneliest melancholy.
>
> "Willing liberates; what means does the will devise for himself to get rid of his melancholy and to mock his dungeon? Alas, every prisoner becomes a fool; and the imprisoned will redeems himself foolishly. That time does not run backwards, that is his wrath; 'that which was' is the name of the stone he cannot move. And so he moves stones out of wrath and displeasure, and he wreaks revenge on whatever does not feel wrath and displeasure as he does. Thus the will, the liberator, took to hurting; and on all who can suffer he wreaks revenge for his inability to go backwards. This, indeed this alone, is what *revenge* is: the will's ill will against time and its 'it was.' "
>
> (*Thus Spake Zarathustra*)

Since the will operates in the temporal world and since time moves only in one direction, the will can never really get at the past. The will's titanic, foredoomed struggle to repeat the past and alter it is simply the revenge that the will seeks for its own impotence in the face of what Nietzsche calls the "it was" of time. Nietzsche connects this revenge against time with the envy that a son feels for his father. In a passage on the equality of men, Zarathustra says,

> "What justice means to us is precisely that the world be filled with the storms of our revenge"—thus they speak to each other. "We shall wreak vengeance and abuse on all whose equals we are not"—thus do the tarantula-hearts vow. "And 'will to equality' shall henceforth be the name of virtue; and against all that has power we want to raise our clamor!"
>
> You preachers of equality, the tyrannomania of impotence clamors thus out of you for equality: your most secret ambitions to be tyrants thus shroud themselves in words of virtue. Aggrieved conceit, repressed envy—perhaps the conceit and envy of your fathers—erupt from you as a flame and as the frenzy of revenge.
>
> What was silent in the father speaks in the son; and often I found the son the unveiled secret of the father.
>
> They are like enthusiasts, yet it is not the heart that fires them—but revenge.

Clearly, the doctrine of the equality of men is at odds with the patriarchal principle that fathers are inherently superior to sons, for obviously the doctrine of equality is the doctrine of a son. The son, finding himself powerless in relation to the father, yet desiring power, admits that mastery inheres in the role of the father but disputes the criteria that determine who occupies that role. The doctrine of the son is simply the doctrine of the son's equality of opportunity to assume the role of the father through a combat with the father that will show who is the better man. But that doctrine of equality the father must reject, for from the father's point of view the authority which he holds as the father is not open to dispute; it is not subject to trial by combat because that authority is not something that the father could ever lose, it is not accidental to fatherhood, it inheres in its very nature. That authority is something which has been irrevocably conferred on the father by the very nature of time, for the essence of the authority, the mastery, that a father has over his son is simply priority in time—the fact that in time the father always comes first. And against that patriarchal authority whose basis is priority in time, the son's will is impotent, for the will cannot move backwards in time, it cannot alter the past. In his rivalry with the father for the love of the mother, the son realizes that no matter how much the mother loves him, she loved the father *first.* Indeed, the son carries with him in the very fact of his own existence inescapable proof that she loved the father first and that the son comes second. Any power that the son has, he has not in his own right, but by inheritance from the father, by being a copy of the father, who has supreme authority because he comes first, who has power because of the very nature of time. No wonder, then, that the envy of the son for the father takes the form of the revenge against time.

When Nietzsche speaks of the "envy of your fathers," the phrase is intentionally ambiguous, for it is not just the envy that a son feels for his father, it is as well the envy that the son inherits from his father, who was himself a son once. The targets of Sutpen's revenge for the affront that he suffered as a boy are the artificial advantages of high birth and inherited wealth (or the artificial disadvantages of low birth and inherited poverty), that is, generation and patrimony—those modes of the son's dependence on his father, those expressions of the fact that whatever the son is or has, he has received from his father and holds at the sufferance of the father. But again we confront the paradox of Sutpen's solution—that he seeks revenge on the artificial standards that make one man inferior to another, not by trying to do away with those standards, but rather by founding a dynasty, by establishing that same artificial standard of superiority for his family and bequeathing it to his son. Put in that way, the paradox seems clearer: it is the paradox that sons turn into fathers by trying to forget (albeit unsuccessfully) that they were once sons. When Sutpen began his quest for revenge, his quest to supplant the father, his attitude was that of a son: that the authority and power of the father obey the rule of power, that they are subject to a trial by combat, and if the son's will proves the stronger, belong to the son not as a gift or inheritance (which would entail his dependence on the father) but as a right, a mark of his independence. Yet (and here is the paradoxical shift) the proof of the son's success in his attempt to become the father will be the son's denial of the attitude of the son (the rule of power) in favor of the attitude of the father. The proof that Sutpen has achieved his revenge, that he has become the father, will be his affirmation that the authority and power of the father obey not the rule of power but the rule of authority, that is, that they are not subject to dispute or trial by combat since they belong irrevocably to the father through priority in time, that to oppose the father is to oppose time, that authority and power cannot be taken from the father by the son but can only be given as a gift or inheritance by the father to the son. We see why Sutpen's revenge requires that he found a dynasty, for the proof that he has succeeded in becoming the father will finally be achieved only when he bequeaths his authority and power to his son as an inheritance (a gift, not a right), thereby establishing the son's dependence on his father and thus the father's mastery. That proof, of course, Sutpen never achieves, though he dies trying. His is the paradoxical fate of one who tries to seize authority and power by one rule and then hold them by another, the fate of a man who wants to be God. Or we could say, shifting the focus slightly, that Sutpen sets out to vindicate the right of every poor white boy to an equal opportunity to become the rich planter, but that once he has vindicated that right by becoming the rich planter, he immediately denies that same right to black boys, specifically, to his black son Charles Bon. We can also see why Faulkner equated Sutpen's attempt to establish that one man cannot be inferior to another through artificial standards or circumstances with his attempt to prove that man is immortal, for if the former attempt aims at toppling that traditional power of the father over the son's life that is implicit in the inherited advantages of position and wealth (or the inherited disadvantages of poverty and lack of position), and if that aim involves the son's challenging that authority of the father whose basis is priority in time so that the son's will directly opposes itself to the nature of time, then that aim can be successful only if the son is able to free himself from the grip of time, only if man can free himself from time's final sanction—death, that inevitable castration of the son by Father Time—only if man can become immortal.

When Sutpen returns from the Civil War to find one son dead and the other gone, he starts over a third time in his design to found a dynasty, to get the son who will inherit his land and thereby prove, through his dependence, that Sutpen has succeeded in his quest to be the son who seized the power of the father and then, as the father, kept that power from being seized by his own son in turn. For Sutpen can only prove that he is a better man than his father if he proves that he is a better man than his son, since Sutpen's father would have been defeated by his son in that very act. In Sutpen's final attempt to achieve his design, the battle against time receives its most explicit statement: "He was home again where his problem now was haste, passing time, the need to hurry. *He was not concerned,* Mr. Compson said, *about the courage and the will, nor even about the shrewdness now. He was not for one moment concerned about his ability to start the third time. All that he was concerned about was the possibility that he might not have time sufficient to do it in, regain his lost ground.*" But then, "*he realized that there was more in his problem than just lack of time, that the problem contained some super-distillation of this lack: that he was now past sixty and that possibly he could get but one more son, had at best but one more son in his loins, as the old cannon might know when it had just one more shot in its corporeality.*" The problem is not just too little time; it is also the physical impotence that time brings, a physical impotence symbolic of Sutpen's "old impotent logic," of the impotence of the son's will in the face of the "it was" of time. Rosa says that when Sutpen gave her her dead sister's wedding ring as a sign of their engagement it was "as though in the restoration of that ring to a living finger he had turned all time back twenty years and stopped it, froze it."

Sutpen's concern that he might be able to get only one more son leads him to suggest to Rosa that they try it first, and if the child is a male, that they marry. That suggestion drives Rosa from Sutpen's home and leads Sutpen to choose for his partner in the last effort to accomplish his design the only other available woman on his land, Milly Jones, the granddaughter of the poor-white Wash Jones, and that choice brings Sutpen to the final repetition of the traumatic affront. In fact, Sutpen had reenacted that affront from the very start of his relationship with Wash Jones, never allowing Jones to approach the front of the mansion. When Sutpen seduces Milly and when her child is a daughter rather than the required son, Sutpen rejects mother and child as he had rejected his first wife and child. He tells Milly that if she were a mare he could give her a decent stall in his stable—a remark that Wash Jones overhears and that makes Jones realize for the first time Sutpen's attitude toward him and his family. Jones confronts the seducer of his granddaughter and kills him with a scythe. The irony of Sutpen's final repetition of the affront is that, though he delivers the affront in the role of a father rejecting his child, in order to get that child he had to assume the role of the son, he had to become the seducer; and Wash Jones, the poor white who had been the object of Sutpen's paternalism, now assumes the role of outraged father in relation to Sutpen. It is emblematic of the fate of the son in his battle against time that Sutpen, struggling in his old age to achieve his revenge, must again become the son and in that role be struck down by an old man with a scythe.

Certainly, the manner of Sutpen's death suggests the iconography of Father Time—that figure of an old man armed with a scythe or sickle for whom all flesh is grass. And it is more than likely that Faulkner intends that this allusion to the figure of Father Time should remind us of the genesis of that figure in mythology, for Father Time is an ancient conflation, based in part on a similarity of names, of two figures—Kronos, Zeus's father, and Chronos, the personification of Time. As we know, that conflation ultimately led to the attachment of at least two of the major legends of Kronos to Father Time—first, that Kronos is a son who castrated his father, Ouranos, and was in turn castrated by his own son Zeus, and second, that Kronos is a father who devours his children. Discussing the evolution of the iconography of Father Time, the art historian Erwin Panofsky notes that the learned writers of the fourth and fifth centuries A.D. began to provide the old figure of Kronos/Saturn with new attributes and "reinterpreted the original features of his image as symbols of time. His sickle, traditionally explained either as an agricultural symbol or as the instrument of castration, came to be interpreted as a symbol of *tempora quae sicut falx in se recurrent*; and the mythical tale that he had devoured his children was said to signify that Time, who had already been termed 'sharp-toothed' by Simonides and *edax rerum* by Ovid, devours whatever he has created" (*Studies in Iconology*).

In discussing the nature of time, Nietzsche alludes to both the legends of Kronos that became associated with Father Time. In the passage from *Zarathustra* in which he talks about the revenge against time, he mentions "this law of time that it must devour its children," and in *Philosophy in the Tragic Age of the Greeks* he says, "As Heraclitus sees time, so does Schopenhauer. He repeatedly said of it that every moment in it exists only insofar as it has just consumed the preceding one, its father, and then is immediately consumed likewise." One might say that the struggle between the father and the son inevitably turns into a dispute about the nature of time, not just because the authority of the father is based on priority in time, but because the essence of time is that in the discontinuous, passing moment it is experienced as a problem of the endless displacement of the generator by the generated, while in the continuity of the memory trace it is experienced as a problem of the endless destruction of the generated by the generator. In this last sense, we refer not just to the experience that what is generated in and by time is as well consumed in and by time, but also to the experience that the price which the generative moment exacts for its displacement into the past is a castration of the present through memory. In tropes such as "the golden age," "the lost world," "the good old days," the past convicts the present of inadequacy through lack of priority, lack of originality, since to be a copy is to be a diminution, because the running on of time is a running down, because to come after is to be fated to repeat the life of another rather than to live one's own.

The struggle between Quentin and his father that runs through the stream-of-consciousness narrative of Quentin's last day is primarily a dispute about time. The narrative begins with Quentin's waking in the morning ("I was in time again") to the ticking of his grandfather's watch, the watch that his father had presented to him, saying, "I give it to you not that you may remember time, but that you may forget it now and then for a moment and not spend all your breath trying to conquer it." Quentin twists the hands off his grandfather's watch on the morning of the day when he forever frees himself and his posterity from the cycles of time and generation. When Quentin is out walking that morning, he passes the shopwindow of a watch store and turns away so as not to see what time it is, but there is a clock on a building and Quentin sees the time in spite of himself: he says, "I thought about how, when you dont want to do a thing, your body will try to trick you into doing it, sort of unawares." And that, of course, is precisely Quentin's sense of time—that it is a compulsion, a fate. For his father has told him that a man is the sum of his misfortunes and that time is his misfortune like "a gull on an invisible wire attached through space dragged." In his struggle against his father and thus against time, Quentin must confront the same problem that he faces in the story of Sutpen and his sons—whether a man's father is his fate. In *Absalom* when Shreve begins to sound like Quentin's father, Quentin thinks, "*Am I going to have to have to hear it all again. . . . I am going to have to hear it all over again I am already hearing it all over again I am listening to it all over again I shall have to never listen to anything else but this again forever so apparently not only a man never outlives his father but not even his friends and acquaintances do.*"

When Quentin demands that his father act against the seducer Dalton Ames, Quentin, by taking this initiative, is in effect trying to supplant his father, to seize his authority. But Quentin's father refuses to act, and the sense of Mr. Compson's refusal is that Quentin cannot seize his father's authority because there is no authority to seize. Quentin's alcoholic, nihilistic father presents himself as an emasculated son, ruined by General Compson's failure. Mr. Compson psychologically castrates Quentin by confronting him with a father figure, a model for manhood, who is himself a castrated son. Mr. Compson possesses no authority that Quentin could seize because what Mr. Compson inherited from the General was not power but impotence. If Quentin is a son struggling in the grip of Father Time, so is his father. And it is exactly that argument that Mr. Compson uses against Quentin. When Quentin demands that they act against the seducer, Mr. Compson answers in essence, "Do you realize how many times this has happened before and how many times it will happen again? You are seeking a once-and-for-all solution to this problem, but there are no once-and-for-all solutions. One has no force, no authority to act in this matter because one has no originality. The very repetitive nature of time precludes the existence of originality within its cycles. You cannot be the father because I am not the father—only Time is the father." When Quentin demands that they avenge Candace's virginity, his father replies, "Women are never virgins. Purity is a negative state and therefore contrary to nature. It's nature is hurting you not Caddy and I said That's just words and he said So is virginity and I said you dont know. You cant know and he said Yes. On the instant when we come to realise that tragedy is secondhand." In essence Quentin's father says, "We cannot act because there exists no virginity to avenge and because there exists no authority by which we could avenge since we have no originality. We are second-hand. You are a copy of a copy. To you, a son who has only been a son, it might seem that a father has authority because he comes first, but to one who has been both a father and a son, it is clear that to come before is not necessarily to come first, that priority is not necessarily originality. My fate was determined by my father as your fate is determined by yours." Quentin's attempt to avenge his sister's lost virginity (proving thereby that it had once existed) and maintain the family honor is an attempt to maintain the possibility of "virginity" in a larger sense, the possibility of the existence of a virgin space within which one can still be first, within which one can have authority through originality, a virgin space like that Mississippi wilderness into which the first Compson (Jason Lycurgus I) rode in 1811 to seize the land later known as the Compson Domain, the land "fit to breed princes, statesmen and generals and bishops, to avenge the dispossessed Compsons from Culloden and Carolina and Kentucky," just as Sutpen came to Mississippi to get land and found a dynasty that would avenge the dispossessed Sutpens of West Virginia. In a letter to Malcolm Cowley, Faulkner said that Quentin regarded Sutpen as "originless." Which is to say, that being without origin, Sutpen tries to become his own origin, his own father, an attempt implicit in the very act of choosing a father figure to replace his real father. When Quentin tells the story of the Sutpens in *Absalom,* he is not just telling his own personal story, he is telling the story of the Compson family as well.

The event that destroyed Sutpen's attempt to found a dynasty is the same event that began the decline of the Compson family—the Civil War closed off the virgin space and the time of origins, so that the antebellum South became in the minds of postwar Southerners that debilitating "golden age and lost world" in comparison with which the present is inadequate. The decline of the Compsons began with General Compson "who failed at Shiloh in '62 and failed again though not so badly at Resaca in '64, who put the first mortgage on the still intact square mile to a New England carpetbagger in '66, after the old town had been burned by the Federal General Smith and the new little town, in time to be populated mainly by the descendants not of Compsons but of Snopeses, had begun to encroach and then nibble at and into it as the failed brigadier spent the next forty years selling fragments of it off to keep up the mortgage on the remainder." The last of the Compson Domain is sold by Quentin's father to send Quentin to Harvard.

Mr. Compson's denial of the existence of an authority by which he could act necessarily entails his denial of virginity, for there is no possibility of that originality from which authority springs if there is no virgin space within which one can be first. And for the same reason Quentin's obsession with Candace's loss of virginity is necessarily an obsession with his own impotence, since the absence of the virgin space renders him powerless. When Mr. Compson refuses to act against Dalton Ames, Quentin tries to force him to take some action by claiming that he and Candace have committed incest—that primal affront to the authority of the father. But where there is no authority there can be no affront, and where the father feels his own inherited impotence, he cannot believe that his son has power. Mr. Compson tells Quentin that he doesn't believe that he and Candace committed incest, and Quentin says, "If we could have just done something so dreadful and Father said That's sad too, people cannot do anything that dreadful they cannot do anything very dreadful at all they cannot even remember tomorrow what seemed dreadful today and I said, You can shirk all things and he said, Ah can you." Since Mr. Compson believes that man is helpless in the grip of time, that everything is fated, there is no question of shirking or not shirking, for there is no question of willing. In discussing the revenge against time, Nietzsche speaks of those preachers of despair who say, "Alas, the stone *I was* cannot be moved," and Mr. Compson's last words in Quentin's narrative are "was the saddest word of all there is nothing else in the world its not despair until time its not even time until it was."

Is there no virgin space in which one can be first, in which one can have authority through originality? This is the question that Quentin must face in trying to decide whether his father is right, whether he is doomed to be an impotent failure like his father and grandfather. And it is in light of this question that we can gain an insight into Quentin's act of narration in *Absalom,* for what is at work in Quentin's struggle to bring the story of the Sutpens under control is the question of whether narration itself constitutes a space in which one can be original, whether an "author" possesses "authority," whether that repetition which in life Quentin has experienced as a compulsive fate can be transformed in narration, through an act of the will, into a power, a mastery of time. Indeed, Rosa Coldfield suggests to Quentin when she first involves him in the story of the Sutpens that becoming an author represents an alternative to repeating his father's life in the decayed world of the postwar South: " 'Because you are going away to attend the college at Harvard they tell me,' Miss Coldfield said. 'So I dont imagine you will ever come back here and settle down as a country lawyer in a little town like Jefferson, since Northern people have already seen to it that there is little left in the South for a young man. So maybe you will enter the literary profession as so many Southern gentlemen and gentlewomen too are doing now and maybe some day you will remember this and write about it.' " We noted earlier that the dialogue between Quentin and his father about virginity that runs through the first part of *Absalom* appears to be a continuation of their discussions of Candace's loss of virginity and Quentin's inability to lose his virginity contained in Quentin's section of *The Sound and the Fury*. Thus, the struggle between father and son that marked their dialogue in *The Sound and the Fury* is continued in their narration of *Absalom*. For Quentin, the act of narrating Sutpen's story, of bringing that story under authorial control, becomes a struggle in which he tries to best his father, a struggle to seize "authority" by achieving temporal priority to his father in the narrative act. At the beginning of the novel, Quentin is a passive narrator. The story seems to choose him. Rosa involves him in the narrative against his will, and he spends the first half of the book listening to Rosa and his father tell what they know or surmise. But in the second half, when he and Shreve begin their imaginative reconstruction of the story, Quentin seems to move from a passive role to an active role in the narrative repetition of the past.

So far I have mainly discussed the experience of repetition as a compulsion, as a fate, using Freud's analysis of the mechanism of the repetition compulsion in *Beyond the Pleasure Principle* as the basis for my remarks. But in that same text, Freud also examines the experience of repetition as a power—repetition as a means of achieving mastery. He points out that in children's play an event that the child originally experienced as something unpleasant will be repeated and now experienced as a source of pleasure, as a game. He describes the game of *fort/da* that he had observed being played by a little boy of one and a half. The infant would throw away a toy and as he did, utter a sound that Freud took to be the German word *fort*—"gone." The child would then recover the toy and say the word *da*—"there." Freud surmised that the child had created a game by which he had mastered the traumatic event of seeing his mother leave him and into which he had incorporated the joyful event of her return. Freud points out that the mechanism of this game in which one actively repeats an unpleasant occurrence as a source of pleasure can be interpreted in various ways. First of all, he remarks that at the outset the child "was in a *passive* situation—he was overpowered by the experience; but, by repeating it, unpleasurable though it was, as a game, he took on an *active* part. These efforts might be put down to an instinct for mastery that was acting independently of whether the memory was in itself pleasurable or not. But still another interpretation may be attempted. Throwing away the object so that it was 'gone' might satisfy an impulse of the child's, which was suppressed in his actual life, to revenge himself on his mother for going away from him. In that case it would have a defiant meaning: 'All right, then, go away! I don't need you. I'm sending you away myself.' "

Freud makes a further point about the nature of children's games that has a direct bearing on our interest in the son's effort to become his father: "it is obvious that all their play is influenced by a wish that dominates them the whole time—the wish to be grown-up and to be able to do what grown-up people do. It can also be observed that the unpleasurable nature of an experience does not always unsuit it for play. If the doctor looks down a child's throat or carries out some small operation on him, we may be quite sure that these frightening experiences will be the subject of the next game; but we must not in that connection overlook the fact that there is a yield of pleasure from another source. As the child passes over from the passivity of the experience to the activity of the game, he hands on the disagreeable experience to one of his playmates and in this way revenges himself on a substitute." Significantly, Freud refers to this mastery through repetition as "revenge," and his remarks suggest that this revenge has two major elements—repetition and reversal. In the game of *fort/da* the child repeats the traumatic situation but reverses the roles. Instead of passively suffering rejection when his mother leaves, he actively rejects her by symbolically sending her away. And in the other case, the child repeats the unpleasant incident that he experienced but now inflicts on a playmate, on a substitute, what was formerly inflicted on him.

In this mechanism of a repetition in which the active and passive roles are reversed, we have the very essence of revenge. But we must distinguish between two different situations: in the idea situation, the revenge is inflicted on the same person who originally delivered the affront—the person who was originally active is now forced to assume the passive role in the same scenario; in the other situation, the revenge is inflicted on a substitute. This second situation sheds light on Sutpen's attempt to master the traumatic affront that he suffered as a boy from the man who became his surrogate father, to master it by repeating that affront in reverse, inflicting it on his own son Charles Bon. This scenario of revenge on a substitute sheds light as well on the connection between repetition and the fantasy of the reversal of generations and on the psychological mechanism of generation itself. The primal affront that the son suffers at the hands of the father and for which the son seeks revenge throughout his life is the very fact of being a son—of being the generated in relation to the generator, the passive in relation to the active, the effect in relation to the cause. He seeks revenge on his father for the generation of an existence which the son, in relation to the father, must always experience as a dependency. But if revenge involves a repetition in which the active and passive roles are reversed, then the very nature of time precludes the son's taking revenge on his father, for since time is irreversible, the son can never really effect that reversal by which he would become his father's father. The son's only alternative is to take revenge on a substitute—that is, to become a father himself and thus repeat the generative situation as a reversal in which he now inflicts on his own son, who is a substitute for the grandfather, the affront of being a son, that affront that the father had previously suffered from his own father. We can see now why Nietzsche, in connecting the revenge against time with the "envy of your fathers" (that envy which the son feels for his father and which the son has inherited from his father, who was himself a son), says, "What was silent in the father speaks in the son; and often I found the son the unveiled secret of the father" (*Thus Spake Zarathustra*).

When Sutpen takes revenge on a substitute for the affront that he received as a boy, he takes revenge not just on Charles Bon but on Henry as well. For if the primal affront is the very fact of being a son, then acknowledgment and rejection, inheritance and disinheritance are simply the positive and negative modes of delivering the affront of the son's dependency on the father. Further, we can see the centrality of the notion of revenge on a substitute to the figure of the double. The brother avenger and the brother seducer are, as I have pointed out, substitutes for the father and the son in the Oedipal triangle, but if the revenge which the father inflicts on the son is a substitute for the revenge that the father wishes to inflict on his own father, then the brother avenger's killing of the brother seducer becomes a double action: the avenger's murder of the seducer (son) is a symbolic substitute for the seducer's murder of the avenger (father). This adds another dimension to Henry's murder of Bon: Henry is the younger brother and Bon the older, and the killing of the older brother by the younger is a common substitute for the murder of the father by the son. Thus, when Henry kills Bon, he is the father-surrogate killing the son, but since Henry, like Bon, is also in love with their sister Judith, he is as well the younger brother (son) killing the older brother who symbolizes the father, the father who is the rival for the mother and who punishes incest between brother and sister, son and mother. The multiple, reversible character of these relationships is only what we would expect in a closed system like the Oedipal triangle, and it is precisely this multiple, reversible character that gives the Oedipal triangle a charge of emotional energy that becomes overpowering as it cycles and builds. The very mechanism of doubling is an embodiment of that revenge on a substitute which we find in generation, for it is the threat from the father in the castration fear that fixes the son in that secondary narcissism from which the figure of the double as ambivalent Other springs. When the bright self (the ego influenced by the superego) kills the dark self (the ego influenced by the unconscious), we have in this murder of the son as related to his mother by the son as related to his father the reversed repetition of that repressed desire which the son felt when he first desired his mother and was faced with the threat of castration—the desire of the son to murder his father. For the psychologically impotent son who cannot have a child, the act of generating a double is his equivalent of that revenge on the father through a substitute which the potent son seeks by the act of generating a son.

Keeping in mind this notion of revenge on a substitute, we can now understand how Quentin's act of narration in *Absalom* is an attempt to seize his father's authority by gaining temporal priority. In the struggle with his father, Quentin will prove that he is a better man by being a better narrator—he will assume the authority of an author because his father does not know the whole story, does not know the true reason for Bon's murder, while Quentin does. Instead of listening passively while his father talks, Quentin will assume the active role, and his father will listen while Quentin talks. And the basis of Quentin's authority to tell the story to his father is that Quentin, by a journey into the dark, womblike Sutpen mansion, a journey back into the past, has learned more about events that occurred before he was born than either his father or grandfather knew:

> "Your father," Shreve said. "He seems to have got an awful lot of delayed information awful quick, after having waited forty-five years. If he knew all this, what was his reason for telling you that the trouble between Henry and Bon was the octoroon woman?"
>
> "He didn't know it then. Grandfather didn't tell him all of it either, like Sutpen never told Grandfather quite all of it."
>
> "Then who did tell him?"

"I did." Quentin did not move, did not look up while Shreve watched him. "The day after we—after that night when we—"

"Oh," Shreve said. "After you and the old aunt. I see. Go on."

In terms of the narrative act, Quentin achieves temporal priority over his father, and within the narrative Quentin takes revenge against his father, against time, through a substitute—his roommate Shreve. As Quentin had to listen to his father tell the story in the first half of the novel, so in the second half Shreve must listen while Quentin tells the story. But what begins as Shreve listening to Quentin talk soon turns into a struggle between them for control of the narration with Shreve frequently interrupting Quentin to say, "Let me tell it now." That struggle, which is a repetition in reverse of the struggle between Mr. Compson and Quentin, makes Quentin realize the truth of his father's argument in *The Sound and the Fury*—that priority is not necessarily originality, that to come before is not necessarily to come first. For Quentin realizes that by taking revenge against his father through a substitute, by assuming the role of active teller (father) and making Shreve be the passive listener (son), he thereby passes on to Shreve the affront of sonship, the affront of dependency, and thus ensures that Shreve will try to take revenge on him by seizing "authority," by taking control of the narrative. What Quentin realizes is that generation as revenge on a substitute is an endless cycle of reversibility in which revenge only means passing on the affront to another who, seeking revenge in turn, passes on the affront, so that the affront and the revenge are self-perpetuating. Indeed, the word "revenge," as opposed to the word "vengeance," suggests this self-perpetuating quality—*re-*, again, + *veneger,* to take vengeance—to take vengeance again and again and again, because the very taking of revenge is the passing on of an affront that must be revenged. We might note in this regard that the repetition compulsion is itself a form of revenge through a substitute. If, as Freud says, the act of repression always results in the return of the repressed, that is, if repression endows the repressed material with the repetition compulsion, and if the repressed can return only by a displacement, can slip through the ego's defenses only by a substitution in which the same is reconstituted as different, then the repetition compulsion is a revenge through substitution, wherein the repressed takes revenge on the ego for that act of will by which the repressed material was rejected, takes revenge by a repetition in reverse, by a return of the repressed that is experienced as a compulsive overruling of the will, a rendering passive of the will by the unwilled return of that very material which the will had previously tried to render passive by repressing it. As revenge on a substitute is a self-perpetuating cycle of affront and revenge, so too repression, return of the repressed, re-repression, and re-return are self-perpetuating. In his work on compulsion neurosis, the psychoanalyst Wilhelm Stekel discusses the case of a patient who reenacted the Oedipal struggle with his father through the scenario of an incestuous attachment to his sister and a struggle with his brother. Stekel notes that the patient's compulsive-repetitive acts were a "correction of the past," and he links this impulse to correct the past to that "unquenchable thirst for revenge so characteristic of compulsion neurotics" (*Compulsion and Doubt*). At one point in the analysis, the patient describes his illness as an "originality neurosis."

In his narrative struggle with Shreve, Quentin directly experiences the cyclic reversibility involved in revenge on a substitute—he experiences the maddening paradox of generation in time. At the beginning of their narrative, Quentin talks and Shreve listens, and in their imaginative reenactment of the story of the Sutpens, Quentin identifies with Henry, the father-surrogate, and Shreve identifies with Charles Bon, the son, the outsider. But as the roles of brother avenger and brother seducer are reversible (precisely because the roles for which they are substitutes—father and son—are reversible through substitution), so Quentin and Shreve begin to alternate in their identifications with Henry and Bon, and Quentin finds that Shreve is narrating and that he (Quentin) is listening and that Shreve sounds like Quentin's father. Quentin not only learns that *"a man never outlives his father"* and that he is going to have to listen to this same story over and over again for the rest of his life, but he realizes as well that in their narration he and Shreve *"are both Father"*—*"Maybe nothing ever happens once and is finished. . . . Yes, we are both Father. Or maybe Father and I are both Shreve, maybe it took Father and me both to make Shreve or Shreve and me both to make Father or maybe Thomas Sutpen to make all of us."* In terms of a generative sequence of narrators, Mr. Compson, Quentin, and Shreve are father, son, and grandson (reincarnation of the father). Confronting that cyclic reversibility, Quentin realizes that if sons seek revenge on their fathers for the affront of sonship by a repetition in reverse, if they seek to supplant their fathers, then the very fathers whom the sons wish to become are themselves nothing but sons who had sons in order to take that same revenge on their own fathers. Generation as revenge against the father, as revenge against time, is a circular labyrinth; it only establishes time's mastery all the more, for generation establishes the rule that a man never outlives his father, simply because a man's son will be the reincarnation of that father. And if for Quentin the act of narration is an analogue of this revenge on a substitute, then narration does not achieve mastery over time; rather, it traps the narrator more surely within the coils of time. What Quentin realizes is that the solution he seeks must be one that frees him alike from time and generation, from fate and revenge: he must die childless, he must free himself from time without having passed on the self-perpetuating affront of sonship.

The Fate of Design

Gary Lee Stonum

As I Lay Dying and *Absalom, Absalom!* occupy parallel positions in Faulkner's career, each of the novels a development of one aspect of the concept of arrested motion. The former . . . is Faulkner's most sustained consideration of the theme of motion. The latter is his most sustained meditation on the activity of arresting. In the referential fiction the characters and the writer himself are also both perforce engaged in arresting motion. *Absalom, Absalom!*, however, marks a significant change in Faulkner's understanding of this characteristic artistic activity. The change can be broadly described by saying that the labor of representation is for the first time in *Absalom, Absalom!* made a part of the text. The novel accordingly puts in question just those referential premises that had enabled Faulkner to write the works of the previous phase. As we shall see in analyzing *Absalom, Absalom!*, this change in turn opens the way for new questions about the purpose of art and its place in the world.

The question of arrest turns in part on the relation of subject to object. Arresting is the means by which the subject represents the object, that is, the world in motion, to himself. Faulkner's understanding that the aim of every artist (and the typical desire of every character) is to arrest motion by artificial means allows for an abrupt distinction between subject and object. The subject can exercise the power to be detached from the world and to regard it as if from across a distance. In the referential fiction the writer always maintains such detachment, and so, frequently, do the char-

From *Faulkner's Career: An Internal Literary History*. © 1979 by Cornell University. Cornell University Press, 1979.

acters. Cash's impersonal consciousness, which watches the sane and the insane doings of the world, is one example. There are a number of others throughout Faulkner's work, in which a character seems to watch the world indifferently—the customary word is "muse"—from the other side of a barrier.

In such instances the techniques of arrest and the resulting forms and concepts by which motion is structured constitute the barrier. Such forms give the subject a means of shaping and processing experience and also of coping with it. For the characters, however, these forms often prove ineffective either as defenses against the turbulent motion or as ways of organizing it. The subject's detachment from motion serves at best to postpone a breathless immersion in it. For example, all of the principals in *Light in August* (but for Lena Grove, who never supposes herself aloof from motion) discover that they cannot maintain their detachment. Hightower's dream of foolhardy glory, Byron Bunch's clock-ordered regimen, and Christmas's desperate flight from society all prove unable to limit motion or to keep the world at bay.

For such characters, the measure of the success of their forms of arrest seems to be a fairly simple one, the adequacy of the form in balancing between the external fluidity and an internal need for stasis and order. For a character to be without adequate means of structuring experience is for him to be threatened by a king of vertigo in the face of unmediated and therefore incoherent fluidity. At night Ike Snopes cannot even "see and know himself to be an entity solid and cohered in visibility instead of the uncohered all-sentience of fluid and nerve-springing terror." Benjy Compson experiences a similar vertigo at the welter of chaotically whirling shapes which appear when he is put under ether and when he is drunk on the wedding champagne. Such moments of crisis for the two idiots are the extremes of formlessness in Faulkner's writings; motion is not arrested at all but experienced with terrifying immediacy.

The common failing among other characters is the opposite, a need for rigid and static forms in which to contain, to understand, and thus to cope with worldly experience. Horace Benbow and Quentin Compson are ready examples of characters who try to barricade themselves against life's motion by refusing to acknowledge all that does not conform to their subjective ideals. Such characters are just as vulnerable to vertigo. Throughout Faulkner's career the climactic recognition scenes depict the panic of such a character at the sudden breakdown of his mental constructs before a flood of menacing experience. The scene in *Sanctuary* in which Horace gazes at the photograph of his niece is an example. A later one is Levine's suicide in *A Fable*.

Yet although the character's attempt to shape and limit the motion of the world usually proves ineffective and his detachment from the world only illusory, Faulkner in the referential novels constantly maintains his own detachment from motion. The impersonal artist gives the appearance of coolly selecting or inventing the artificial forms that arrest the motion of the world in his text. His relation to the world and to the text is one of mastery over an external thing. The first criterion for the writer's success seems to be the same as for the character's ability to cope with motion. Successful literary forms strike a balance between the fluid disorder of the world and the transcendent stasis of the writer's viewpoint. The difference is that the writer's stasis is never seriously threatened by the fluidity across the barrier. His detachment from the world and his mastery over it allow the striking of a balance to belong to the purest and most sanitary formalism. Craft and technique are only "tools," as Faulkner sometimes later called them. They can be picked up or discarded as the occasion demands, without ever being invested with any real existential significance to the writer or any power over him.

The situation is never quite this simple, to be sure. Even in the referential fiction, success in striking a balance between order and disorder or stasis and motion is only the most elementary measure of a writer's forms and techniques. The point is that even this elementary measure becomes highly problematic in *Absalom, Absalom!* In that novel the writer's arrest of motion is no longer allowed to depend even initially or primarily on the formalistic, emotionally neutral deployment of tools.

The novel also insists upon one of the writer's tasks in arresting motion which goes beyond those he shares with Darl Bundren and Quentin Compson. In addition to coping with the motion of the world, the writer seeks to make an artifact which will represent that world. Arresting and shaping as the work of creating a product—a dynasty, a historical narrative, or a book—are central to *Absalom, Absalom!* as they never are in the novels of the previous phase. Only in such isolated incidents as the furniture dealer's story in *Light in August* do the characters of the referential novels seek to produce narrative accounts of the world like their creator's.

The term in *Absalom, Absalom!* which gathers the several meanings of arrest, production, and form is "design," Thomas Sutpen's word for his plans and ambitions. The word can be construed in three different ways, as an *intention*, an *act*, and a *pattern*. Each of these is relevant to the novel and to its significance in Faulkner's career. A design is first an intention toward that which is to be shaped; Sutpen and his chroniclers all have designs upon the material before them. Used in this way, the noun signifies the preexisting relationship between a designer and his material. As a verb, design stands for the act of shaping, Sutpen's continuing implementation of his plans or the narrators' struggles to produce an account of his life. And finally, again as a noun, a design is a result, the shape the designer has produced or the pattern into which he has transformed the material.

The problem of design in *Absalom, Absalom!* manifests itself in the seeming failure of every attempt at it. Sutpen's intention to create a dynasty ends in ruin; the narrators' attempts to shape Sutpen's story are confused and uncertain; and Sutpen and the narrators all confess their failure to find a pattern that will allow them to explain what has happened. Quentin, after insisting that Shreve would have to be born in the South to understand, admits that he doesn't understand either. Rosa Coldfield has for forty years been asking "*Why and Why and Why.*" Mr. Compson confesses of his own design for the story that "it just does not explain." Even Sutpen admits in the bifurcated account of his life to General Compson that he can't discover his mistake.

In the earlier fiction the analogy between the arresting activities of the characters and those of the artist is largely a way of conceiving the significance of human endeavor. In *Absalom, Absalom!* the direction of the analogy is reversed. The representation of the characters' attempts to shape their own lives and, especially, to compose narrative accounts of experience becomes a way of interrogating art. Faulkner does not here exempt himself, as he does earlier, from the conditions that govern his fictional world. His representational activities are not privileged over those of his narrators, nor does he adopt the impersonal, godlike viewpoint which had characterized the earlier novels. Sutpen's design is a crucial part of the novel's self-interrogation, but the most immediate question for the writer is the relationship of the narrators' designs and the design of the novel. What is at stake in designing a narrative, and why are the characters so unable to compose one that satisfies them? Can the novel be said to succeed where the narrators have failed, and if so, what would it mean for the novel's design to be called successful? What, in short, is the measure of successful design?

The mere asking of such questions marks a change in Faulkner's career, for it draws into the open the enabling principles of the previous phase. . . . *Absalom, Absalom!* is in part an exploration of questions uncovered in the closing pages of *As I Lay Dying.* A rather tidy developmental logic connects Cash's final monologues to the concern in *Absalom, Absalom!* with composing an account of past—rather than immediate, ongoing, and incomplete—experience. But the links between the two novels bespeak more differences than similarities. The most important premise of *As I Lay Dying,* the writer's ability to represent fully the inner lives of his characters, is what the writer and the narrators seem least able to assume in *Absalom, Absalom!*

Although by Faulknerian standards of verisimilitude, *Absalom, Absalom!* is a realistic enough novel—probably more so than *As I Lay Dying*—it is not particularly a referential work in the sense in which I have been using the term. It is not simply an impersonal representation of a theme, the question of design, which happens to be more self-reflexive than Faulkner's earlier themes. (The theme is not in fact noticeably more reflexive or self-referential than some of the themes in *As I Lay Dying*. However, the earlier novel's concern about language really operates only at the level of the characters' representational activities.) *Absalom, Absalom!* is not, in other words, an imitation of the question of design as rhetorically posed by a writer who yet stands behind his novel in serene and confident mastery and by this stance refuses the application of the question to his own design. Rather, the asking of the question demands the establishment of a new set of relationships among the writer, his material, and the particular design of his text.

Although we can be reasonably sure that the narrators' designs fail, it is not so easy to say where the inadequacies lie. They are not particularly to be found in the patterns that govern each narrator's account. As Olga Vickery has shown, these patterns are in large part those of distinct literary genres: Greek tragedy, the Gothic tale, and chivalric romance (*The Novels of William Faulkner*). Mr. Compson's version of the story can perhaps be criticized as too willfully rigid an application of the form of Greek tragedy, but he is the first to point out that his design is unsatisfactory. More interestingly, the pattern itself is far more compelling than Mr. Compson is ever allowed to say. Faulkner admitted as much years later when he identified Sutpen's destruction with "the old Greek concept of tragedy."

Mr. Compson's narrative founders on the arbitrariness of casting Charles Bon as an embodiment of fate. Compson calls him an "effluvium of Sutpen blood and character" in a desperate attempt to make sense of his "impenetrable and shadowy character." But of course he is more than an effluvium; we eventually learn that he is Sutpen's repudiated black son and thus a perfectly convincing representative of the nemesis necessarily raised by Sutpen's hubristic design. A similar case can be made for the adequacy of Rosa's Gothic demonizing. Faulkner originally planned to entitle the novel "Dark House," and its Gothic machinery is not solely a product of Rosa's imagination. The burning of Sutpen's mansion, for example, is an appropriately Gothic conclusion which she never gets to narrate.

Rosa's demonizing expresses her need to relegate Sutpen to the realm of the supernatural, and this need derives chiefly from what she insists is the one lasting outrage he has committed against her. Raised to consider him an ogre and later deeply shocked by his proposal for a trial breeding, she asserts to Quentin that she has nonetheless forgiven him all but one thing, his having died and thus put himself forever beyond the reach of her questions. Sutpen as demon is thus not so much the definitive pattern Rosa affirms for the story as the "zero signifier" she invokes for the inexplicable excess of meaning in it (Claude Lévi-Strauss, "Introduction to the Work of Marcel Mauss"). Or rather, to use a term more appropriate to Rosa's sensibility, "demon" serves her in much the same way the trope "infinity" serves Poe, Rosa's most illustrious southern predecessor as a sentimental poet and teller of Gothic tales. "This, like 'God,' 'spirit' and some other expressions of which equivalents exist in all languages is by no means the expression of an idea—but of an effort at one. It stands for the possible attempt at an impossible conception" (Edgar Allan Poe, "Eureka").

Mr. Compson's design for the story uses fate—"Fate, destiny, retribution, irony—the stage manager, call him what you will"—in the same way, as a sign of the inexplicable. The uncanny machinations of fate are for Mr. Compson the very pattern of the events, even as he admits: "It's just incredible. It just does not explain." He, in fact, uses inexplicability and his own failure to explain as the confirmations of his design. "Or perhaps that's it: they dont explain and we are not supposed to know. . . . You bring them together again and again nothing happens: just the words, the symbols, the shapes themselves, shadowy inscrutable and serene, against that turgid background of a horrible and bloody mischancing of human affairs."

The patterns that Mr. Compson and Rosa offer for the story are simultaneously forms which confess their failure to find a truly satisfactory form and designs which are more cogent than either narrator is able to say. This anomalous situation may suggest to us that the essential criteria for design are to be found not in the patterns but in the personal limitations of the designers and the ways in which they apply otherwise compelling forms. In a statement often quoted as an authoritative commentary on the novel's status as an exercise in multiple perspective, Faulkner argues just that.

> I think that no one individual can look at truth. It blinds you.
> You look at it and you see one phase of it. Someone else looks
> at it and sees a slightly awry phase of it. But taken all together,

the truth is in what they saw though nobody saw the truth intact. . . . The old man was himself a little too big for people no greater in stature than Quentin and Miss Rosa and Mr. Compson to see all at once. It would have taken perhaps a wiser or more tolerant or more sensitive or more thoughtful person to see him as he was. It was, as you say, thirteen ways of looking at a blackbird. But the truth, I would like to think, comes out, that when the reader has read all these thirteen different ways of looking at the blackbird, the reader has his own fourteenth image of that blackbird which I would like to think is the truth.

Read as an epistemological credo, the statement gives with one hand what it takes away with the other. Faulkner begins by asserting a radical relativism: no one can see truth. But he also characterizes the novel as a way of overcoming relativism. The reader is supposed to do what no individual can. And the writer, who reassures us in these words that some whole truth exists, necessarily commands the same powers to comprehend truth, just as he does in *As I Lay Dying*.

Read less rigorously, as a suggestion of the moral qualities one needs to design a true image, the statement points to other difficulties. Perhaps the reader (and the writer) can be expected to be wiser or more tolerant than Shreve and Quentin, say, who have much the same task as the reader in assembling a composite image out of "old tales and talking." To read Faulkner's statement in this way encourages us to give over looking for truth in designs and images themselves; it licenses us to scrutinize instead the moral qualities inherent in how the narrators go about their acts of designing. By understanding their personal failings, we can be expected to be directed toward nobler and more effective methods of composing a fourteenth image. Again this suggests the mode of *As I Lay Dying* or *The Sound and the Fury*, where the reader is allowed to share the writer's objectivity and to inspect from above the failings of Addie's or Jason's strategies for arresting motion.

Such modes of analysis, however, are likely to lead to the uncomfortable conclusions reached by James Guetti in a study which is otherwise the most thorough consideration of the problem of design in this novel (*The Limits of Metaphor*). Although he does not cite Faulkner's comment about the fourteen ways, Guetti pursues the arguments that both an epistemological and a moral reading of it would suggest. He insists that Faulkner means to show in the novel the necessary and inevitable failure of design—in Guetti's terms, of metaphor. *As I Lay Dying* can, for example, surely be said to demonstrate the inevitable failure to arrest the motion of present experience and to offer a reasonably full explanation of why it is inevitable. But Guetti finds that failure in *Absalom, Absalom!* results on the one hand from unexplained and perhaps inexplicable premonitions of failure, silence, and darkness and on the other from the idiosyncratic qualities of the designers. In both cases Faulkner's own design is flawed. Either the writer cannot articulate the significance of the darkness that Guetti shows to be an essential part of both Quentin's and Sutpen's imaginations, or else the novel speaks only of the circumstantial and thus finally insignificant difficulties that these particular unwise, intolerant, and insensitive narrators find themselves in and so offers the reader precious few insights about how to design successfully.

The gap between a vague but universal failure of design and one that seemingly proceeds from very specific but local and unrepresentative circumstances—Mr. Compson's want of information, for example—is the result of the paradox Guetti wants to see at the heart of the book, a paradox which is a version of the Cretan liar's dilemma. According to Guetti, Faulkner means to design a novel which demonstrates that all designing fails. But Faulkner's own inevitable failure produces an incoherent text that Guetti must reluctantly conclude is "no novel at all."

Looking for the failure of design either in the narrative patterns or in the character of a narrator and the way this conditions his act of designing produces readings that show, directly or indirectly, the similarities between *Absalom, Absalom!* and the more univocally referential works. Both kinds of analysis finally objectify the text; that is, they examine it as a self-contained second world which has a relatively straightforward mimetic relationship to our primary world. There are many good reasons for reading *Absalom, Absalom!* in this way, and I do not mean to suggest that, for example, to read the novel as a fictional representation of southern history will lead one inescapably into logical paradox. My purpose in suggesting the limitations of such analysis is to clarify by contrast the difference between the enabling assumptions of *Absalom, Absalom!* and those of earlier novels. Rather than assuming or stipulating a relationship between the world of the text and the world of reality, Faulkner in *Absalom, Absalom!* is specifically trying to *establish* such a relationship. But this relationship proves to be as risky and uncertain as the one between the South, which Quentin is asked to tell about, and the narrative of the Sutpen family he offers in response.

The enabling assumptions of *As I Lay Dying* include a first world discovered to be significant because of men's attempts to arrest its turbulent flow, an instrumental language which can represent men's consciousness of the world, and a writer who is able to detach himself from the world in order to represent it objectively and impersonally. *Absalom, Absalom!* questions all these assumptions. It does so partly by insisting upon the remaining meaning of design: design as intention, or rather as the intentional relationship between the designer and his material, the designs he has upon it and those it has upon him.

One aspect of the circumstantiality that bothers Guetti is in fact a crucial element in this relation between designer and material. It is precisely the local, in William Carlos Williams's sense of the term, which grounds the problem of design and removes it from the realm of abstract formalism. To the characters in the referential novels, by contrast, the question of arrest usually is abstract. Darl Bundren's attachment to "some concept, some shape of beauty" is precisely the desire to subordinate the concrete local detail to an abstract form.

In *Absalom, Absalom!,* for the writer as well as for the characters, the local is what preexists the self, what is inherited from the past. . . . To regard the past is to be faced with something no longer characterized by motion. Cash and the narrators of *Absalom, Absalom!* are seeking to design a flux that has solidified or precipitated. The past assumes the aspect of something substantive or material. And in becoming material, the past becomes much the same kind of thing as the worldly literary materials which a writer engages.

For Faulkner the two essential properties of literary material are just these. Literary material is a substance, and it is inherited by the writer because of his living in a certain time and place. Both properties are crucial to the problem of design. Faulkner often insists on the materiality of what he has been given to write about. His material is the South, "my little postage stamp of native soil," a body he invariably refers to in synecdochic figure as land and earth and soil. The image is not of men's doings or a historical tradition or a culture but of the land itself. In *Absalom, Absalom!* the image is on virtually every page: the "tranquil and astonished earth" which Sutpen overruns, the "land or earth or whatever it was that destroyed Sutpen at last," the "land" which Sutpen advises the Klan to attend to if the South is to be saved, and even the Continental Trough which links Quentin and Shreve: "that River which runs not only through the physical land of which it is the geologic umbilical, not only runs through the spiritual lives of the beings within its scope, but is very Environment itself."

Language, the writer's medium, is itself an inherited materiality. In a pair of early essays Faulkner contrasts what he sees as the meager achievement of the American writer with his fortunate situation as the heir to the "wealth of natural dramatic material in this country, the greatest source being our language" ("American Drama: Eugene O'Neill" and "American Drama: Inhibitions," *Early Prose and Poetry*). American speech has a distinctively "earthy strength" that the writer must learn to appropriate. In this otherwise ordinary metaphor, language itself appears as palpably material and thus a quite different thing from the transparent medium of representation it is in *As I Lay Dying*. The failing of American literature, Faulkner asserts, is that it is as yet "inarticulate." The earthy material has not yet been well articulated, not yet properly divided up and set in order. Such an inadequacy is a failure of design.

Each of these concepts and images operates in *Absalom, Absalom!*, where the difficulties of appropriating one's material inheritance are explored in full. To exist in the world of the novel, for example, is to be *"a certain segment of rotted mud,"* or a *"narrow delicate fenced virgin field,"* or *"articulated flesh."* All of the narrators find in the Sutpen story material intimately connected with Southern heritage. For Quentin especially, this heritage prominently includes the language in which it is bequeathed to him; everyone, it seems, *"sounds just like father."* The story itself is primarily a tale of inheritances. Sutpen and his descendants all live in a world where fathers customarily bequeath difficult burdens to their children.

The central problem of design in *Absalom, Absalom!* is the relationship between a designer and an inherited body of material, a relationship that largely constitutes both the material and the designer as such. Subject and object exist not as truly independent entities but by virtue of a relationship which defines them both. Quentin is not "a being, an entity" but a "commonwealth," the sum of his relationships to the "ghosts" of the past. He never really confronts the material for a first time but only remembers it. *"But you were not listening, because you knew it already, had learned, absorbed it already without the medium of speech somehow from having been born and living beside it, with it, as children will and do: so that what your father was saying did not tell you anything so much as it struck, word by word, the resonant strings of remembering."* Likewise, for Rosa Coldfield the *"unpaced corridor which I called childhood"* and the *"Cassandralike listening beyond closed doors"* which figuratively portray the relation to her inheritance have taught her *"to listen before I could comprehend and to understand before I even heard."* The common situation of Sutpen in trying to establish a dynasty, of Charles Bon in seeking the recognition of a father, of Quentin Compson in trying to tell about the South, and of the writer in composing a novel is to exist by virtue of an already established relationship to inherited material.

From the point of view of the designer of a life, a historical recitation, or a novel, this relationship is the way in which he apprehends his inherited material before he actually begins to design it. This mode of apprehension is what I have also called the intention of a design and what Husserlian phenomenology would designate more rigorously as an intentional structure. It largely determines the fate of design as act and as pattern. For example, Mr. Compson's act of casually designing the tale as an amusing if somewhat bizarre after-dinner story and the tragic pattern he finds in it both belong to the relationship already established between him and the southern past. From the outset he assumes his own age to be permanently alien to the simple and foolhardy heroics "of that day and time, of a dead time; people too as we are, and victims too as we are, but victims of a different circumstance, simpler and therefore, integer for integer, larger, more heroic and the figures therefore more heroic too, not dwarfed and involved but distinctive, uncomplex."

The novel's most important image of a relation to what preexists poses Sutpen and Quentin directly against the inherited materiality of earth. For Sutpen at the moment his design is born, the earth is a "limitless flat plain" against which his "innocence" rises "like a monument." (This scene is the closest thing in the book to a representation of the primordial moment when the relation between designer and material initially gets constituted.) In contrast, Quentin, as he rides out to the Sutpen house with Rosa finds himself enclosed within the substance of his world and thwarted by it.

> The dustcloud in which the buggy moved not blowing away because it had been raised by no wind and was supported by no air but evoked, materialized about them, instantaneous and eternal, cubic foot for cubic foot of dust to cubic foot for cubic foot of horse and buggy, peripatetic beneath the branch-shredded vistas of flat black fiercely and heavily starred sky, the dust cloud moving on, enclosing them not with threat exactly but maybe warning, bland, almost friendly, warning, as if to say, *Come on if you like. But I will get there first; accumulating ahead of you I will arrive first, lifting, sloping gently upward under hooves and wheels so that you will find no destination but will merely abrupt gently onto a plateau and a panorama of harmless and inscrutable night and there will be nothing for you to do but return and so I would advise you not to go, to turn back now and let what is, be.*

These two images of a character's relationship to earth depict also the two necessary and reciprocally opposed relationships to materiality of the novelist himself. The first, utter detachment from material which is assumed to be so much unformed and pliable stuff, is an assumption of mastery. It allows the writer to command his material just as Sutpen speaks "the *Be Sutpen's Hundred* like the oldentime *Be Light*." The second is a recognition of helplessness, a realization that one does not speak the material so much as listen to it and be spoken by it. The writer in composing the novel—as the composing of the novel—enacts both relationships. He is at all points trying to effect "some happy marriage of speaking and hearing" which might surpass the differences between them. If the text stands as that marriage, however, it is more truly an amalgamation of the two relationships than a synthesis of them into a third, encompassing perspective.

The only place where the differences between the two relationships do seem truly to be surpassed is the one region where they have not yet come into being, the mountain paradise where Sutpen is born. There in a country beyond history and almost beyond culture—if culture be defined as differentiation, categorization, and articulation—one's relationship with land is harmonious, "because where he lived the land belonged to anybody and everybody." The young Sutpen "had never even heard of, never imagined, a place, a land divided neatly up and actually owned by men." What is at stake in design—Sutpen's, Quentin's and the writer's—is possession. As in *Go Down, Moses* the initial possession of the land is the origin of history and civilization. It is the act of original sin, Promethean theft, and godlike creation which founds the opposition between nature and culture. For the writer, to whom this opposition appears as that between his material and what he makes of it, as that between reality and fiction, the composition of the novel is his attempt to take possession of the material for fiction.

Sutpen's story begins with a fall from the communal Eden. (The mythic interpretation is explicit in the narrative Quentin has inherited from his grandfather.) On the journey down to tidewater Virginia, the earth itself seems to be the agent transforming Sutpen's relation to it: "They did not seem to progress at all but just to hang suspended while the earth itself altered." The fall and the new relation to earth reveal two things to Sutpen. One is the fact that he has a heritage which conditions his own life: "All of a sudden he discovered, not what he wanted to do but what he just had to do, had to do it whether he wanted to or not, because if he did not do it he knew that he could never live with himself for the rest of his life, never live with what all the men and women that had died to make him had left inside of for him to pass on, with all the dead ones waiting and watching to see if he was going to do it right." The other is the specific character of his inheritance from his poor-white father as one of the "cattle, creatures heavy and without grace, brutely evacuated into a world without hope or purpose for them."

Both these discoveries arise out of his being turned away from the plantation owner's door, and they result eventually in his lifelong endeavor to repudiate the inheritance and replace it with one of his own design. That endeavor is of course an act of awesome and hubristic will, but it is important to note that the exercise of will and the design itself both follow the establishment of a relationship between self and substance which then allows the will its freedom. The young Sutpen's final discovery in his lengthy debate with himself proceeds from the conclusion that no relation at all exists between himself and the plantation owner to the vision of earth as a *tabula rasa*. "*There aint no good or harm either in the living world that I can do to him.* It was like that, he said, like an explosion—a bright glare that vanished and left nothing, no ashes nor refuse; just a limitless flat plain with the severe shape of his intact innocence rising from it like a monument." The designing will finds room in which to work only with the belief in its self-contained alienation from the social order and with the corresponding belief that the world is but clay in wait of the sculptor's tool or a blank page awaiting inscription.

These beliefs are the foundation of Sutpen's innocence and the enabling principles of his design. Sutpen's relationship to the limitless flat plain never changes; he continues to believe from then on that material—the land, the social order, other persons—can be shaped according to his design. "It was that innocence again, that innocence which believed that the ingredients of morality were like the ingredients of pie or cake and once you had measured and balanced them and mixed them and put them into the oven it was all finished and nothing but pie or cake could come out." Even as the narrator of his own life story Sutpen is aloof from the material, almost indifferent to it: "He was not talking about himself. He was telling a story. He was not bragging about something he had done; he was just telling a story about something a man named Thomas Sutpen had experienced, which would still have been the same story if the man had had no name at all, if it had been told about any man or no man over whiskey at night."

This passage accurately depicts also the intentional relationship between writer and material in the referential novels. It is undoubtedly more truthful to say, however, that it describes the result, in which the writer has achieved the desired impersonality, than his process of composition. Even in 1933, only two years after he had proclaimed the value of impersonality and four years after he had written *As I Lay Dying,* his most impersonal work, Faulkner argued that the process of writing could never be impersonal for a Southerner. "That cold intellect which can write with calm and complete detachment and gusto of the contemporary scene is not among us." Sutpen's desired mastery over his material nevertheless duplicates and puts in question the apparent mastery of *As I Lay Dying*. It might be argued that Sutpen represents only an extreme exaggeration of the will to power over one's material, but Faulkner has upon occasion expressed a similar hubris. "I can move these people around like God, not only in space but in time too."

The Failure of Sutpen's design shows the inadequacy of such a relationship to material. Sutpen's relationship is, in fact, not simply inadequate but false to the actual state of affairs. Contrary to his beliefs, Sutpen cannot help but be related to the plantation owner and to the social order represented by him. Likewise, the land is not a *tabula rasa*. The proof of Sutpen's error lies in the double bind that follows upon his attempt to vindicate the little boy at the door. He can only make sure that any "nameless stranger" and his descendants are welcomed in and thus "riven forever free from brutehood just as his own (Sutpen's) children were" by turning away his eldest son. The instruments with which he combats the plantation owner—"land and niggers and a fine house"—are not neutral materials with which he can create a cosmos out of the "soundless Nothing." They are not, that is, like the tools Faulkner sometimes thinks his literary techniques to be. They are materials which have already been designed and which retain the power to shape the user in their own image. Sutpen even seems for a moment, as Quentin tells it, to realize the shaping power of materiality when he speaks of needing "to have what they have that made them do what the man did." The supposedly neutral materials, in other words, prove to be the implements of a social order that Sutpen necessarily winds up repeating rather than repudiating or transforming.

Quentin has no such innocence about the materials of his heritage. His relationship to the ghosts of the southern past dictates not that he design them but that they design him in their own image. If Sutpen's freedom to design his life is largely an illusion founded on his innocence about the power of inherited materiality. Quentin's "freedom" is "that of impotence." He can only recognize helplessly that he has been made into the "Quentin Compson who was still too young to deserve yet to be a ghost, but nevertheless, having to be one for all that, since he was born and bred in the deep South." The other Quentin Compson also, the one "preparing for Harvard," who may yet have some hope of designing his own life, discovers that even in Massachusetts he cannot escape "listening, having to listen." "*I am going to have to hear it all over again I am already hearing it all over again I am listening to it all over again I shall have to never listen to anything else but this again so apparently not only a man never outlives his father but not even his friends and acquaintances do."* This passage follows Quentin's protest to Shreve that "I am telling." But Quentin's fate, one he comes to recognize fully, is always to listen to the material and never to speak it.

Quentin is so often and so casually referred to as the principal narrator of the novel, especially of the second half of the book, that it is important to recognize just how little he speaks. Excluding what is merely thought and seen by Quentin but uttered by the third-person narrator and ignoring remarks of a sentence or two, Quentin "speaks" only sixty pages of the 378-page novel. What Quentin does say is repeatedly characterized as second- or thirdhand transmission of the words of his father, General Compson, or Thomas Sutpen. All of his spoken narrative is in chapter 7, where he punctuates his discourse with "father said" and "grandfather said" so frequently that Shreve virtually parodies him at one point. "I see. Go on. And father said——." Cleanth Brooks's chart of the main conjectures made about the Sutpens reveals the same thing. Only one of the forty or so can be attributed to Quentin (*William Faulkner: The Yoknapatawpha Country*). Quentin does, after some resistance, assent to the romance motif introduced by Shreve, but he never really offers a pattern of his own. In fact, with the crucial exception that his story is meant to *"tell about the South,"* he can hardly be said to intend a design at all.

But of course a design does get spoken in his share of the novel. In one respect it is a conglomeration of all the ghostly voices which have spoken previously. Yet Quentin's design emerges most fully from the scenes that he alone cannot help but hear and see. "He could see it; he might even have been there. Then he thought *No. If I had been there I could not have seen it this plain.*" The power of Quentin's relationship to material is that he is so deeply enclosed within it and submitted to it that he can see and know it more intimately than anyone else. Only Quentin can discern the element that most fully explains the story, the secret of Bon's birth. Many critics have been bothered that this knowledge seems to have no source. They usually want to see the discovery of the secret conform to the kind of designing they understand Quentin to be practicing, "that best of ratiocination which after all was a good deal like Sutpen's morality." Such critics are therefore forced to assume that Quentin has been told by Henry or Clytie and that Faulkner somehow neglected to inform us of this most essential incident. But as Shreve realizes, Quentin learns of Bon's identity just by entering the house for the first time and standing face to face with one of Sutpen's children. "She didn't tell you, it just came out of the terror and the fear after she turned you loose. . . . She didn't tell you in the actual words because even in the terror she kept the secret; nevertheless she told you, or at least all of a sudden you knew."

Intimate knowledge of material comes only from submitting oneself to it and being shaped by it. Quentin's passivity, his "sullen bemusement," is as necessary for a successful design as the power of will exercised by Sutpen and belatedly even by Rosa, who "refused at the last to be a ghost." Whereas Sutpen's assumption of mastery over the earth allows him the will to design it but at the same time constitutes his "purblind innocence," Quentin's awareness of the "weightless permeant dust" moving "sluggish and dry across his sweating flesh" allows him the power of vision and forecloses the power of will.

What is at stake in the question of design is the possibility of successfully appropriating one's heritage. It is apparently not possible to refuse the question. Bon, who at first thinks that "no man had a father," discovers that he must spend his life seeking recognition from a father "out of the shadow of whose absence my spirit's posthumeity has never escaped. Bon and Henry represent another important pair of relationships to inheritance, the one seeking to establish recognition that he has a father and the other borne down by the burden of a father's command. For the writer, however, the problem of design is chiefly manifested in Quentin and Sutpen.

In one respect the problem of design and inheritance is a theme represented in the novel by the actions of the Sutpens, Coldfields, and Compsons. But the novel is not only the representation of action but a kind of action itself, the enactment of the writer's appropriation of the South as literary material. Both submitting to his material and striving to establish mastery over it, Faulkner seeks to make it his own in a way quite different from that he had peremptorily used in the referential novels. The boldest assertion in the book is the signature to the map in its endpapers. "William Faulkner: Sole Owner and Proprietor." As the inscriptions on this map make clear, the act of appropriation extends beyond *Absalom, Absalom!* to include all the Yoknapatawpha County fiction yet composed. It extends even into the future in the reference to the then unpublished (and probably unwritten) story of Flem Snopes as a bank president. But the confidence displayed on the map should not obscure the fact that *Absalom, Absalom!* presents a kind of art in which the writer's proprietorship over his material is less likely to be secured than strived for or at best tenuously maintained.

The crucial problem of design in the novel, then, is not the detached writer's deployment of forms that can adequately mediate between order and disorder. It is the prior question of establishing a relationship to one's material which then makes the use of such forms possible but which at the same time forecloses the possibility of true detachment. In Geoffrey Hartman's terms the writer's relation to the *genius loci* takes priority over his relationship to Genius ("Towards Literary History," *Beyond Formalism,* New Haven, 1970). The writer's relation to native materials and his capacity both to command them and to submit to the claims they make upon him takes precedence over form as such and over the writer's place in a tradition of literary forms.

Absalom, Absalom! and most of the novels that follow after it differ from the referential works in a number of prominent ways. The three most important of these are all related to the new centrality of the writer's relationship to inherited materials. The first is the significance of history. Faulkner's reputation as a writer who is obsessed with the past may obscure the fact that he is, until 1936, chiefly a novelist of the contemporary scene. Until *Absalom, Absalom!* history figures in the novels primarily as a background against which his characters strive to cope with the motion of the contemporary world. But nine of the eleven novels published after 1935 are wholly or largely historical, and they are centrally concerned with taking possession of an inheritance or with relinquishing one.

Another difference, which first appears in the 1935 *Pylon,* is Faulkner's adoption of a new style, the one that is normally and rightly thought of as characteristically Faulknerian: the use of long sentences and complex, suspended constructions. As Faulkner explained a number of times, the style is his attempt to get the past into the present. "A man, a character in a story at any moment of action is not just himself as he is then, he is all that made him, and the long sentence is an attempt to get his past and possibly his future into the instant in which he does something." In other words, the style is explicitly a means of taking possession of the past. Moreover, it serves the writer as a means of personally appropriating his material. Whereas the ideal in the referential works had been artistic impersonality and the style had accordingly been much less of a signature, a characteristic style is by definition personal, even in Faulkner's case idiosyncratic. It manifests the writer's necessarily personal attempt to take possession of his material and to mark it permanently as his own.

The final and most important difference is the relation of the representational act to the resulting representation. In *Absalom, Absalom!* the result, the finished book, includes the act, the attempt to take possession of the material and to shape it in some definitive form. Rosa Coldfield, the only character in the novel who is a writer, gives us several metaphors for the act of representation and describes the attendant relationships among designer, material, and designed product when she speaks of *"that sickness*

somewhere at the prime foundation of this factual scheme from which the prisoner
soul, miasmal-distillant, wroils ever upward sunward, tugs its tenuous prisoner
arteries and veins and prisoning in its turn that spark, that dream which, as the
globy and complete instant of its freedom mirrors and repeats (repeats? creates,
reduces to a fragile evanescent iridescent sphere) all of space and time and massy
earth, relicts the seething and anonymous miasmal mass." The achieved dream—
a dynasty or a work of art—is necessarily a mirror and a repetition of the
massy earth. But it is not created primarily to be a truthful representation
or an object of aesthetic contemplation. It is the means by which the prisoner
soul strives to create itself as a free and distinct being. Like Thomas Sutpen,
the writer struggles to create himself and his freedom as distinct from the
anonymous earth and connected to it by a relation of mastery. But, like
Quentin, he knows also that he must always remain a prisoner of that massy
materiality and that he cannot create a new earth, only repeat the old one
in fragile, evanescent, iridescent sphere.

One may read an exalted conception of art in Rosa's words; it lies in
the capacity of art to attain a kind of permanence. The prisoner soul *"dies,*
is gone, vanished: nothing," but its representation of the earth "relicts" the
material in permanent form. Faulkner's use of "relict" as a verb has a precise
function here. It combines two related but distinguishable ideas. One is the
notion of giving something up and getting free from it; "relinquish" is the
word Faulkner normally uses for this idea by itself. The other is the notion
of leaving behind a relict which survives. The prisoner soul thus makes a
survivor of the representation as he leaves it and the massy earth behind.

In repeating the world, giving a design to its material and arresting its
motion in the palpable form of a house, a social structure, or a novel one
leaves "a mark on something that *was* once," which may then pass to the
"stranger" Judith speaks of in giving Bon's letter to Mrs. Compson. The
stranger has the name and the same function, it seems, as the stranger who
is to read Faulkner's novels one hundred years hence, according to the 1955
definition of art as arrested motion. In fact, art is for Faulkner man's most
permanent "creation of something . . . which will outlast him." A man
"can't live forever. He knows that. But when he's gone somebody will
know he was here for his short time. He can build a bridge and will be
remembered for a day or two, a monument, for a day or two, but somehow
the picture, the poem—that lasts a long time, a very long time, longer than
anything."

Such lofty sentiments as these likely seem quite at odds with the bleak
tone of *Absalom, Absalom!* But the novel is, in fact, made primarily according
to principles of design which would allow for such a belief in art's power.

The principles I have been explicating do not, however, go unchallenged in the novel. Having traced Faulkner's ideas about proper design from the initial and relatively simplistic notion of form as a balance between stasis and fluidity to the more paradoxical requirement that the writer must both speak his material and be spoken by it, we must now pay attention to those aspects of the novel that call the paradoxical requirement into question. A further scrutiny of Rosa's words in the passage quoted above will show how *Absalom, Absalom!* opens itself to a critique of the principles it otherwise firmly maintains. Her words undercut the novel less directly than do Cash's in *As I Lay Dying,* but they serve the same function in pointing the way to the problem on which the next moment in Faulkner's career will center. What comes into question is not the method of design but its purpose and its consequences.

Rosa is not talking about art in the passage I have quoted but rather of her own reluctance to face the sickness somewhere at the prime foundation of things. She is at this point firmly committed to the *"might-have-been which is more true than truth,"* that is, to a romantic dream which entirely escapes such striving against massy materiality. The struggle against materiality which she deems herself incapable of is also a highly romantic notion, and we must ask whether the novel supports it fully.

The most problematic aspect of Rosa's discourse is her depiction of earth as a chaotic, formless materiality. The concept resembles Sutpen's assumptions about earth, except that Rosa sees materiality not as a neutral resource but as an almost actively malevolent and corrupt miasma. Unformed materiality cannot really be corrupt, however, because there is no such thing as a primal miasma in *Absalom, Absalom!* One's material inheritance is always already inscribed with the cultural designs made upon it by earlier prisoners: designs that include the incest taboo, the plantation system, and Greek tragedy. The question that plagues Quentin, after all, is not how to design an adequate representation of the Sutpen story or even how to understand it, but how to live amid the dusty wreckage of the designs which have been bequeathed to him. The continuing malign power of these designs over his life and the similar power of already existing designs over the lives of Sutpen and his family suggest that the carriers of corruption are designs themselves, not materiality. The sickness is to be found not at the prime foundation of things but in the productions and representations that may ensue from the struggle with materiality.

If this is so, Faulkner's sentiments about the permanence of art are not so much lofty as frightening. Writing a novel like *Absalom, Absalom!* may answer the methodological question with which we began—how to design successfully—but writing a novel that represents and thus repeats sickness may be only a way of transmitting the disease. The permanence of art may be not a virtue but a crime, for it perpetuates the contamination more effectively even than Sutpen's abortive dynasty.

Rosa's language thus leads to a new problem of design, one which ultimately needs to be seen in a context wider than that of this one novel. To recognize that designs may themselves be diseases that infect the generations to come is to have moved beyond the initial question about how one might design successfully. This question is answered, though only in paradox, by the exploration of the intentional relationship to inherited materiality. One must somehow both speak it and be spoken by it. The text of *Absalom, Absalom!* is itself an answer to this question to the extent that it advances a considerable distance toward the paradoxical goal in its circling, tortuous, and fully self-aware articulations.

The new problem is primarily a question neither of one's relation to materiality as such nor of whether that materiality is conceived to be formless, pliable, corrupt, or already potent with design. The intentional relation to materiality is the one which makes new designs and productions possible, and the enabling power of this relationship generally continues to be assumed throughout the rest of Faulkner's career. The new problem is the relationship between designs, the relationship, that is, between one's own productions and the forms of the past. To recall Hartman's distinction once more, this is the writer's position with respect to Genius. Faulkner now begins to ask if there is some way in which one's own designs can be more than a perpetuation of past forms and a conveying into the future of whatever disease they carry. He asks the question, for example, through Ike McCaslin, who in *Go Down, Moses* tries to escape the curse his ancestors' designs have brought upon the land.

Mildly comforting replies to such a question can be seen in the two novels which follow *Absalom, Absalom!* Bayard Sartoris in *The Unvanquished* does manage to transform the code of violence that his father and the war have bequeathed to him. More ambiguously, Harry Wilbourne in *The Wild Palms* manages to proclaim bravely that *"between grief and nothing, I will take grief."* But in *Absalom, Absalom!* itself the fate of design is always ruinous. Most of the characters in the novel are faced with the same predicament as the writer; all need to produce designs that will have a healthy relationship to the designs of the past. Sutpen, who recognizes the design of the plantation system but thinks he can replace it with his own creation, winds up repeating it instead. Quentin, who is fully aware of the designs of the past and the power they wield, remains silent and unproductive in an attempt to avoid accepting such tragic knowledge. Sutpen's heirs, especially the descendants of Charles Bon, are generally ignorant of their situations as inheritors of the design. Their lives are merely dispersed across the land and without a witting relation to a past or a future; they grow up without fathers and their sons are all soon orphans.

The designs of the past thus get furthered in *Absalom, Absalom!* in exactly the ways which . . . are the principal threats to a healthy career; repetition, silence, and dispersion. The parallel is no coincidence. The fate of design and the trajectory of a career are fundamentally similar phenomena; both operate as historical processes and as open systems. Their essential mode of being therefore includes a relation to the past and a relation to the future. The recognition of this parallel between a literary career and social and cultural history is the foundation of the next phase of Faulkner's writing. By considering in this next phase the fate of a particular culture's designs, Faulkner in fact raises the course of his own career to the level of an explicit theme in his fiction.

William Faulkner: Innocence Historicized

Carolyn Porter

> *But the spectacle is not identifiable with mere gazing, even combined with hearing. It is that which escapes the activity of men, that which escapes reconsideration and correction by their work.*
>
> GARY DEBORD

As the critical record demonstrates, we respond to the maddening puzzle of *Absalom, Absalom!* most often in one of the two ways suggested by Mr. Compson's response to the equally maddening puzzle of Sutpen's life: "It's just incredible," he complains, "It just does not explain. Or perhaps that's it: they don't explain and we are not supposed to know." The effort to explain leads to detective work. "Something is missing," as Mr. Compson put it, "you bring them [the characters and their acts] together in the pro-portions called for" by the "chemical formula," but "nothing happens; you reread, tedious and intent, poring, making sure that you have forgotten nothing, made no miscalculation . . . and again nothing happens." In par-ticular, the effort to verify Quentin's knowledge about Bon has led to some elaborate poring over the text, "tedious and intent," in the effort to find that something which is missing. But even when the effort to explain takes on more judicious proportions, to order and comprehend the tragic di-mensions of Sutpen's story, it cannot finally account for the telling of that story except by an appeal to imagination's superiority over reality—which amounts in the end to confessing that we are not supposed to know. On this view, Quentin and Shreve deliver up a "poem of the act of the mind

From *Seeing and Being: The Plight of the Participant Observer in Emerson, James, Adams, and Faulkner.* © 1981 by Carolyn Porter. Wesleyan University Press, 1981.

in the act of finding what will suffice." No doubt they do. No reader can fail to notice that Quentin and Shreve create both the richest and the most convincing version of the story. But it is not sufficient to assert that they succeed because they use their imaginations more energetically than Rosa or Mr. Compson. We need to ask why they are able to do so, and to call upon the transcendental imagination is merely to restate the question, not to answer it. In effect this appeal to the imagination represents the reader's romantic transcendence, while the detective's response reflects his insistence on neutral objectivity, both of which postures, as it happens, Sutpen embodies and ought to contaminate. The options available to the reader are apparently exhausted by Walter Slatoff's frank admission that we are not supposed to know, not because the imagination accounts for what reason fails to explain, but because Faulkner couldn't bring himself to work it all out. I would suggest that none of these responses is finally appropriate, because the novel's strategy is designed to block both subjective and objective escape hatches from history as the stream of event. Nor does Faulkner's novel reflect any final and irremediable incoherence in his own narrative procedures; rather, it reveals the incoherence and contradictions within the society he portrays, as well as in the society he addresses. In short, though I would agree with Cleanth Brooks's staunch insistence that the novel forms a coherent whole. I would support this claim on different grounds. . . .

In *Absalom, Absalom!* [Faulkner] forces the reader to share the burden of narrative construction actively. That is, by casting the novel's central action as an exercise of the imagination in narrative construction, Faulkner implicates his reader as a participant in the telling of a story, a strategy which serves to alter the reader's relation to the novel much as a cubist painting alters the viewer's relation to illusionist space. If, as John Berger argues [in "The Moment of Cubism"], the content of the cubist painting is "the relation between seer and seen," and this painting does not so much illustrate as posit a historical situation, *Absalom, Absalom!* may be said to be about the relationship not only between Quentin Compson and Thomas Sutpen, but also between the reader and the novel. As such, it does not depict a series of scenes on canvas so much as it posits a historically grounded dilemma. Our tendency to conceptualize the novel as a series of versions, as if it were essentially structured like *The Sound and the Fury,* is itself a response whose validity Faulkner has deliberately undermined. His strategy relies primarily on an opposition between sight and hearing, between pictures and voices, and it is designed not only to undercut the stability of any fixed, external vantage point, but to close the gap between seer and seen, between words as printed on a page, and words as uttered in the physical medium of air. . . . Faulkner's strategy works against not the inherent temporality of narrative, but the inherent spatiality of the book— that spatiality which endows the reader with the freedom to "re-read, tedious and intent, poring" over pages which he can turn backward as well as forward. This freedom derives from the simple fact that the reader holds an object in his hand. He can not only reread passages he has already read; he can actually put the book down, rise from his chair, and walk away, out of the talking, the telling. It is this material spatiality which Faulkner sets out to undermine, in order to make of the reader—that emblematic figure of detachment from the "real" world—a participant in the story he reads. The result is a novel in which the protagonist, or at least the only living breathing one in the novel, sits for an entire evening, and for three chapters, "quite still, facing the table, his hands on either side of the open text book . . . his face lowered a little, brooding."

In conventional terms, one could say that the reader becomes a narrator, and because the major line of action in the novel consists in narration itself, the reader is threatened with becoming a character as well. But it seems more accurate to say that the novel is itself one voice in a dialogue with the reader, who, like Quentin Compson, struggles in vain to secure a detached position from which to assemble and confront a chaotic and in-explicable set of events.

It is common to regard Shreve as the surrogate for the reader, since he is the outsider, the one who shares our amazement and incredulity at the story of Sutpen. I would not dispute this claim, but would emphasize the fact that Shreve's voice is first heard on page nine of the novel, where the "two separate Quentins" address each other. If Shreve represents the reader's interests, he does so as an interlocutor in a conversation which functions to relate him intimately to Quentin. In addition to producing a story, Shreve and Quentin verbally consummate a marriage, and when Shreve issues his prophecy in the novel's final chapter, he severs a rela-tionship at the same time. We ought, in short, to find our identification with Shreve rather uncomfortable. Further, Quentin is also a reader sur-rogate, and the best means of approaching Faulkner's strategy is to appre-ciate his dilemma. By remaining a passive hearer, Quentin tries to secure a detached perspective on the story of Sutpen, and so to free himself from the burden of history in which he is already, as a college freshman, en-meshed. But when Shreve assumes the voice of one of the "two separate

Quentins," Quentin is forced to participate in the telling of Sutpen's story, a process which, for a brief hour in the novel's eighth chapter, issues in the "happy marriage of speaking and hearing," only to subside once again in the ninth, leaving Quentin within history as a stream of event, and Shreve outside, measuring and calculating its direction.

Quentin's position is established in the novel's opening chapter. Before Miss Coldfield ever speaks directly, we join Quentin as he listens to her

> talking in that grim haggard amazed voice until at last listening
> would renege and hearing-sense self-confound and the long-dead
> object of her impotent yet indomitable frustration would appear,
> as though by outraged recapitulation evoked, quiet inattentive
> and harmless, out of the biding and dreamy and victorious dust.

Faulkner gradually shifts Quentin's mode of apprehension from hearing to see ("Her voice would not cease, it would just vanish") until Quentin's mind is wholly absorbed by a vision of Sutpen: "Out of quiet thunderclap he would abrupt (man-horse-demon) upon a scene peaceful and decorous as a schoolprize water color." A picture abrupts before Quentin like a slide projected on a screen, a picture of Sutpen "immobile, bearded and hand palm-lifted," surrounded by the wild blacks and the captive architect. Then Quentin seems "to watch" as "out of the soundless Nothing," Sutpen's Hundred is created, the "*Be Sutpen's Hundred* like the oldentime *Be Light.*" In this "soundless" vision even God's words have become objects, seen and not heard. Again, a few pages later, and "as though in inverse ratio to the vanishing voice," the "ghost . . . began to assume a quality almost of solidity, permanence," an "ogre-shape which, as Miss Coldfield's voice went on, resolved out of itself before Quentin's eyes the two half-ogre children." Ellen, "the fourth one," joins the picture now, one in which the four of them are "arranged into the conventional family group of the period," and which finally becomes a "fading and ancient photograph . . . hung on the wall behind and above the voice and of whose presence the voice's owner was not even aware." By page twenty-one, Rosa herself as a child has joined the "musing and decorous wraiths" whom Quentin continues to visualize: "Quentin seemed to watch resolving the figure of a little girl, in the prim shirts and pantalettes . . . of the dead time."

Quentin visualizes the ghosts, then, as Hightower looking through his window once gazed out upon his grandfather's Confederate raid, and in the same way Ellen Coldfield visualizes her family, once Bon has married Judith in her imagination:

She seemed to have encompassed time. She postulated the elapsed years during which no honeymoon had taken place, out of which the (now) five faces looked with a sort of lifeless and perennial bloom like painted portraits hung in a vacuum.

Just as Rosa's conception of Charles Bon "was a picture, an image" because Rosa was "not listening" to what Ellen told her, Quentin's conception of Sutpen and his family is also a picture, because he is not listening to Rosa, but instead watching ghosts resolve before him out of the dust. Most importantly, because Quentin is engaged in ghost-watching, he too seems "to have encompassed time," as he notices that "the sun seemed hardly to have moved." The story Rosa is telling has for him the "quality of a dream," occurring "stillborn and complete in a second" even though he knows that "the very quality upon which it must depend to move the dreamer (verisimilitude) to credulity" is an "acceptance of elapsed and yet-elapsing time." Because Quentin already knows part of the Sutpen story, "the talking, the telling" of it simply strikes "the resonant strings of remembering," issuing in pictures which "encompass" events but do not explain them. And it is because they seem to deny, to stand beyond the realm of "elapsed and yet-elapsing time" that these pictures have a "quality strange, contradictory and bizarre; not quite comprehensible." In other words, Quentin detaches himself from "the telling," which goes on in time, and confronts the images beyond "the voice," the ghosts who manifest "an air of tranquil and unwitting desolation . . . as if" they "had never lived at all."

The opposition established in the novel's opening chapter—between light and the vision it supports, on the one hand, and "moving air" and the talking and hearing it sustains, on the other—is grounded in one more basic, that between transcendence of, and immersion in, the stream of event. The association between vision and the effort to encompass and transcend time finds its definitive expression in Thomas Sutpen. As his first appearance indicates, Sutpen inhabits a realm defined by light. He is imagined at the inception of his design as looking "ahead along the undivulged light rays in which his descendants who might not even ever hear his (the boy's) name, waited to be born," and again "after he would become dead, still there, still watching the fine grandsons and great-grandsons springing as far as the eye could reach." Moreover, he is usually remembered as if he *had* transcended time. For example, when he first arrives in Jefferson, he seems literally to be a "man who came from nowhere": the men on the hotel gallery simply

> looked up, and there the stranger was. He was already halfway
> across the Square when they saw him, on a big hard-ridden roan
> horse, man and beast looking as though they had been created
> out of thin air and set down in the bright summer sabbath
> sunshine in the middle of a tired foxtrot.

Sutpen, it seems, has a habit of "abrupting" upon any scene he comes upon;
further, he is seen as a man who is himself primarily a seer, a demonic
visionary who set out once and forever to transcend time by founding a
dynasty, and he commands the visionary response he gets precisely because
of his remorseless dedication to transcendence, his "indomitable spirit."
"He was the light-blinded bat-like image of his own torment" according
to Rosa Coldfield, who shares his "impotent yet indomitable frustration,"
and accordingly mirrors his typically rigid and upright posture. He is
preeminently the man on a horse, always appearing rigidly erect. With "his
pale eyes . . . at once visionary and alert," he embodies at one and the same
time the transcendent seer and the calculating observer. "Even while riding," Quentin's grandfather says, Sutpen

> was still bemused in that state in which he struggled to hold
> clear and free above a maelstrom of unpredictable and unrea-
> soning human beings, not his head for breath and not so much
> his fifty years of effort and striving to establish a posterity, but
> his code of logic and morality, his formula and recipe of fact
> and deduction whose balanced sum and product declined, re-
> fused to swim or even float.

Sutpen's legalistic "code of logic," his innocent conviction that "the ingredients of morality were like the ingredients of pie or cake," which, once
"measured" and "balanced" and "mixed" could produce "nothing but pie
or cake," marks him as the detached spectator of his own destiny, a figure
whose reified consciousness is signaled by eyes both "ruthless and reposed."
Sutpen's ruthless pursuit of immortality, like Rosa Coldfield's ruthless narrative treatment of Sutpen as Demon, derives from a quest for revenge,
and expresses an "impotent and static rage."

Rosa's rage results from what she describes at one point as the "final
clap-to of a door between us and all that was, all that might have been—a
retroactive severance of the stream of event." Thomas Sutpen's affront
leaves Rosa fixed behind "a sheet of glass" from which she observes "all
subsequent events transpire as though in a soundless vacuum," leaving her
"immobile, impotent, helpless." That "might-have-been which is more

true than truth" then becomes "the single rock we cling to above the maelstrom of unbearable reality." Thomas Sutpen too confronts the clap-to of a door, an affront which leads to a design whose purpose and effect is to "shut that door himself forever behind him on all that he had ever known." Sutpen's design is conceived in an experience of impotence, at the moment when he hears himself saying of the plantation owner, "*I not only wasn't doing any good to him by telling it or any harm to him by not telling it, there ain't any good or harm either in the living world that I can do to him.*" As Sutpen himself admits, the "boy symbol was just a figment of the amazed and desperate child" who is sent to deliver a message and finds that it "*can't even matter*" whether it was delivered or not. To defy this impotence, Sutpen conceives of a design which hypostatizes it, beyond "the living world." Like Rosa Coldfield's dream, Thomas Sutpen's innocence lifts him above the stream of events, from which the "severe shape of his intact innocence" rises as a "monument," to transcend rather than redeem the affront, to order his life in accord with a static design. But Sutpen's design fails for the same reason that God's did; to order time and thereby fill it with meaning, one must inhabit it. God could amend the error by sending his Son into the world, but Sutpen, after trying and failing to imitate God, remains to be "articulated in this world." To appreciate Sutpen's failure, as well as his peculiar immortality, we need to understand the principle which opposes transcendence in the novel.

The clearest explanation of this principle is to be found in Judith Sutpen's single recorded speech. When she gives Bon's letter to Quentin's grandmother, she contrasts her purpose with her father's in bringing home those two colossal tombstones to mark the family grave. The letter differs from the tombstone because the act of passing something on "from one hand to another" represented in the letter

> at least . . . would be something . . . something that might make a mark on something that *was* once for the reason that it can die someday, while the block of stone can't be *is* because it never can become *was* because it can't ever die or perish.

The act of passing on a letter from one hand to another affirms the continuity of life from one generation to the next, and stands as the physical, palpable link between past and present. The letter functions like the "churinga," which Claude Lévi-Strauss describes as an object passed on from one generation to the next in certain tribes, to furnish "the tangible proof that the ancestor and his living descendents are of one flesh" (*The Savage Mind*). As Judith explains, it is a matter of making an "impression." You try at first to make it by weaving a pattern, but "you are born at the same time with a lot of other people," and they are all "trying to make a rug on the same loom only each one wants to weave his own pattern into the rug." You know that "it can't matter," and yet "it must matter because you keep on trying," but then in the end "it doesn't matter," since you die. So much for transcendence. Consequently, Judith responds to impotence—the failure to make an impression which led her father to build a static monument— with the simple physical act of passing something on to someone. Put schematically, Judith thereby allies herself with time as horizontal motion, while Sutpen asserts a vertical transcendence of time. Moreover, Judith's contrast with her father is emphasized by the fact that the letter itself embodies the same principle as the act of passing it on; it is a message passed on from "one mind to another" and in particular, passed from brother to sister, reconnecting the blood relation Sutpen had denied, many years after he had failed to pass on a message. Bon's letter, as well as Judith's act, manifests physically the principle of social continuity at work in all the conversations in the novel. All the speaking and hearing, dominated as it is by a single narrative voice, represents an ongoing social act which, though it cannot found a dynasty, can create a community among the living as well as between the living and the dead.

In contrast to Judith's acceptance of membership in the human community, Sutpen in effect abandons that community when he leaves his family for the West Indies. Accepting her own impotence, Judith nonetheless accepts the responsibilities Sutpen has denied: when she takes in Bon's son at Sutpen's Hundred, she does not know he is in fact her nephew, in contrast to Sutpen who presumably knows that Bon is his son but turns him away just the same. But then Sutpen does not so much deny as fail even to recognize his responsibilities, for his discovery of his own impotence as a boy prohibits him from discovering that his actions can matter in "the living world," with flesh-and-blood people who breathe the same air he does. He thus remains impervious not only to any possible pain he might cause that cannot be paid for legalistically, but also to the reasons for any possible damage done to his design by other people. What makes his actions so offensive to the citizens of Jefferson is that same innocence which makes his failure so inexplicable to Sutpen himself; just as he enters the town as a "man who came from nowhere," so the acts of those who frustrate his design seem to him to come from nowhere. He fails to understand that his actions have effects which outrun his intentions, that is, because he does not recognize intentionality in others. He is a "foe" who does not even know that he is "embattled."

And yet it is because he is embattled that he endures; the counterdesigns provoked by his affronts destroy his design, but ensure his eventual articulation. The central irony of Sutpen's life is that he wins immortality not by achieving his design, which ends in the mocking figure of Jim Bond, but through the counterdesign of one whom he affronts. For it is Rosa who, although she too has revenge in mind, initiates a dialogue with the youth Quentin, and so keeps Sutpen alive. Like the architect he impresses into his service, those whom Sutpen fails to acknowledge as social creatures sharing the same world and breathing the same air with him, create of "Sutpen's very defeat the victory which, in conquering, Sutpen himself would have failed to gain."

It remains to note, before returning to Quentin, that the "moving air" from which Rosa's room is protected becomes Faulkner's vehicle for moving from present to past, and for referring the shift to that stream of events moving outside Rosa's blinds. Moving air serves the same purpose that the sound of insects does in *Light in August,* but functions in a more complex way. At the beginning of chapter 2, the air "still breathed" in 1909 is the "same air in which the church bells had rung on that Sunday morning in 1833," providing Faulkner with a means for modulating into the past without calling attention to the shift. The purpose is similar to that fulfilled by "memory believes before knowing remembers," but here it is achieved by reference to a material, rather than to an abstract, substratum. As Rosa remarks, "there is no such thing as memory: the brain recalls just what the muscles grope for." Air also carries the smell of wisteria and the sound of sparrows into Rosa's office, just as it carries "the wisteria, the cigar-smell, the fireflies–attenuated up from Mississippi" to a strange room in Cambridge, joining North and South, Canadian and American, in a materially grounded social bond. Most important, air carries the sound of human voices, and so acts as the medium in which all the novel's conversations exist. Air sustains life, the physical, palpable life of breathing, smelling, hearing, and even speaking—and thus joins the "sensuous human activity" which is history to the "stream of event" constituted by the voices in the novel.

As we have seen, Quentin resists listening to Rosa, since, as he eventually realizes, he has "had to listen too long." The story of Sutpen is "a part of his twenty years' heritage of breathing the same air and hearing his father talk about the man Sutpen." And so, when Shreve begins retelling it in chapter 6, Quentin thinks *"He sounds just like father,"* registering once again that growing realization that he has had to listen to too much. But as he hears Shreve tell it again, he is drawn out of his detached vantage point. Recounting his father's story of Sutpen's troops bringing the marble tombstone back to Mississippi during the war, Quentin at first follows his habit of viewing: "It seemed to Quentin that he could actually see them." But when Sutpen is seen arriving home with the tombstone, Quentin's habit is undercut: "he could see it; he might even have been there. Then he thought *No. If I had been there I could not have seen it this plain.*" Once Quentin begins to speak, to share in the telling, he is in fact participating in the stream of event for the first time in the novel.

When Quentin starts talking, Shreve remarks, "Don't say it's just me that sounds like your old man," forcing Quentin now to stumble forth from his fixed detachment and acknowledge a relation to Sutpen other than that of seer and seen:

> Yes, we are both Father, or maybe Father and I are both Shreve, maybe it took Father and me both to make Shreve or Shreve and me both to make Father or maybe Thomas Sutpen to make all of us.

Quentin's image of pools attached to one another by a "narrow umbilical water-cord" represents his attempt to conceptualize the community he is about to enter, a community not merely joining him to Shreve, but to his father, and Charles and Henry and Sutpen too. Like that "fierce, rigid umbilical cord" which joins Rosa to Clytie at the moment they touch, the two of them "joined by that hand and arm which held" them, Quentin's image represents the community of blood, "the immortal brief recent intransient blood" shared by the two youths in their tomblike room and by those other two, whom they are soon to join, "riding the two horses through the iron darkness" of a Mississippi Christmas Eve, sixty years before.

Immersed with Shreve, then, in the process of communal telling, Quentin no longer stares at static pictures, but participates in the stream of event, and in an act of love as well, that "happy marriage of speaking and hearing wherein each before the demand, the requirement, forgave condoned and forgot the faulting of the other." But this impassioned telling finally subsides, and when it does, Quentin must face what he saw behind that door, and so fulfill the dust cloud's prophecy: that he will "find no destination but . . . a plateau and a panorama of harmless and inscrutable night and there will be nothing . . . to do but return." All that Quentin testifies to learning from Henry Sutpen is that he has come home to die. Having waited until the last chapter for this confrontation, the reader is met with nothing more than a conversation which mirrors itself:

And you are—?
Henry Sutpen.
And you have been here—?
Four years.
And you came home—?
To die. Yes.
To die?
Yes, to die.
And you have been here—?
Four years.
And you are—?
Henry Sutpen.

What the reader confronts in this passage is an issue to which we will turn shortly. What Quentin confronts here is death, the maddening rebuttal to all designs for transcendence and immortality, and this, of course, is the message of the dust cloud as well. Born into time, man struggles to deny his mortality by transcending the stream of event, but the dust is victorious, as the two rooms in which the novel's opening and closing conversations take place indicate.

From Rosa's room to this one at Harvard, from September to December, Quentin has had to listen to the voices of others, each one "trying . . . to weave his own pattern into the rug," using language itself to try to transcend and encompass time, and each one failing. Thus Quentin and Shreve's dialogue is "a good deal like Sutpen's morality and Miss Coldfield's demonizing," in that each represents the effort of the "prisoner soul" which "coils ever upward sunward" to rise above the earth where time and death await them. Yet, on the other hand, Shreve and Quentin, in their joint act of creation, have accomplished what no one else in the novel could have, and this because they do it together, in an act of love, not vengeance. They use language, too, although not primarily to impose a design, but rather as

> that meager and fragile thread . . . by which the little surface corners and edges of men's secret and solitary lives may be joined for an instant now and then before sinking back into darkness where the spirit cried for the first time and was not heard and will cry for the last time and will not be heard then either.

Yet for a brief hour, Quentin and Shreve do hear and respond. Their act of telling, in other words, differs from those of Rosa Coldfield and Mr. Compson not merely because they imagine more creatively, and so "encompass" more than either, but because of what makes this more ambitious vision possible—their joint participation in the telling, that "happy marriage of speaking and hearing" which not only allows each to forgive the other's faultings, but even enables each to take the other "up in stride without comma or colon or paragraph," voicing that relentless Faulknerian sentence which represents the stream of event in *Absalom, Absalom!*

But their immersion in this stream is brief and passing. It culminates in the closing pages of chapter 8, appropriately enough in a conversation, one between Henry Sutpen and Charles Bon, each played by Quentin and Shreve jointly, since "both of them were Henry Sutpen and both of them were Bon." This dialogue foreshadows the one between Quentin and Shreve at the novel's end, for each dramatizes a confrontation. Bon invites Henry to shoot him; Henry replies, "You are my brother," and Bon responds with the novel's ur-sentence: "No I'm not. I'm the nigger that's going to sleep with your sister. Unless you stop me Henry." Henry, "panting and panting," jerks the pistol from Bon's hand and points it at him, but all that explodes are words: "You shall not!" At the end of the next and final chapter, Shreve, like Bon, throws down his own peculiar gauntlet, asking Quentin, "Why do you hate the South?" and Quentin, "panting in the cold air, the iron New England dark," replies "at once, immediately: 'I dont hate it.' " Furthermore, Shreve has just articulated the results of Henry's impotence as the brother avenger who fails to stop his black brother from sleeping with his white sister: "the Jim Bonds are going to conquer the western hemisphere," he announces, proceeding to echo Bon once more when he says, "in a few thousand years, I who regard you will also have sprung from the loins of African kings." John Irwin has provided a full and convincing treatment of the psychological bases of Quentin's identification with both Bon and Henry. What concerns us here is the split which occurs in both of these dialogues—in the first between brothers, and in the second between two boys who have been joined by a "marriage of speaking and hearing." When Shreve issues his prophecy, he is, like Bon, effectively challenging Quentin with a cold deduction of the consequences to follow from his impotence. While Shreve uses Bond to clear the "ledger," Quentin can still "hear" Bond wailing, unredeemed and unredeemable like Quentin himself as he whispers, "Nevermore of peace." At the novel's end, Quentin's two selves have split apart irrevocably; Quentin has fallen into the "fluid cradle of events (time)" where death lies waiting, while Shreve steps neatly forth to make his predictions. Furthermore, Shreve's summing-up parodies the attempt on the part of the reader to stand off and assemble a final interpretation, to detach himself from the talking, the telling.

From the beginning, Faulkner has been immersing us in the stream of event which his sustained voice embodies. His strategy in this respect consists in telling us things before we can understand him, possessing us of information before we have learned where it fits in the story, while at the same time pulling us forward by withholding the crucial information about Bon's past, as well as the crucial scene in which we expect to have this information verified. By the end of chapter 1, for example, we actually know about the major events of Sutpen's life after his arrival in Jefferson, although we cannot make sense of them. As a result, when these events are related again and again in the ensuing chapters, we know them "already," so that what is said almost seems to strike, as it does for Quentin, "the resonant strings of remembering." Further, as we read on, it is as if we, like Quentin, had been brought into a room and experienced a shock at the sight of Sutpen abrupting before us, as if we "knew" but did not yet "believe" what we had seen. And because we, like Rosa, were not there to see these events, we visualize them for ourselves, much as we visualize the static picture of Rosa and Quentin in that vividly presented opening scene.

By the time we reach the end of chapter 5, the events Rosa has conjured up before us have, thanks to Quentin's father, been placed in some sequence, but they remain for us, as for him, like Quentin's pictures, "contradictory and bizarre," because we still lack the information which will account for them, the facts about Charles Bon's past. "Something is missing," as Mr. Compson puts it, that something which our "chemical formula" has failed to include, so that when we bring the characters together "in the proportions called for . . . nothing happens." This kind of scrutinizing of the events one has witnessed and the account one has made of them is precisely the kind of activity in which we find Sutpen himself engaged in the second half of the novel, as he sits

> there in Grandfather's office trying to explain with that patient amazed recapitulation, not to Grandfather and not to himself . . . but trying to explain to circumstance, to fate itself, the logical steps by which he had arrived at a result absolutely and forever incredible, repeating the clear and simple synopsis of his history . . . as if he were trying to explain it to an intractible and unpredictable child.

Like Rosa Coldfield, Sutpen sits in an office addressing himself not to his interlocutor, but to "fate itself." Further, the story as Sutpen tells it provides an excellent example of that "idealization," as Heisenberg calls it, "in which

we can speak about parts of the world without any reference to ourselves."
For Sutpen depicts himself as acting wholly out of his obligations to the
design in his mind—that "pure idea" which Emerson had once invited his
reader to make the world conform to—and the result is a carefully controlled
series of denials: "I did not undertake—I did not even demand. . . . I accepted
them . . . I could have reminded them . . . but I did not; . . . I merely
explained . . . I made no attempt . . . I declined and resigned all right and
claim that I might repair whatever injustice I might be considered to have
done by so providing for the two persons whom I might be considered to
have deprived of anything I might later possess." It is hardly surprising
that General Compson cannot go on listening to this recital after Sutpen
refers to his "conscience," for there is no conscience in evidence here, no
capacity for recognizing responsibility or guilt, but instead the demonstra-
tion of an innocent belief that immunity can be bought from the bonds of
flesh and blood.

Unlike Shreve and Quentin during the climactic chapter 8, where
Shreve exhibits a manifest need to meet Quentin's repeated complaint,
"that's still not love," participating in a joint struggle to come up with an
account of Bon and Judith, Thomas Sutpen addresses no one but himself.
And he virtually treats his failed design as if it were itself a book, over
which he pores, "tedious and intent," trying to locate the missing fact he
had forgotten, the "mistake" he had made, so as to explain "a result absolutely and forever incredible." Shreve's summing-up is contaminated by
the same resolute insistence on clearing the whole "ledger" and so is Mr.
Compson's effort to combine "the words, the symbols, the shapes" standing out against "that turgid background of a horrible and bloody mischancing of human affairs" by means of a "chemical formula." For Mr.
Compson resorts essentially to a romantic interpretation of the puzzle he
cannot fit together in any other way: Sutpen and his family lived in a now
"dead time," he says,

> people too as we are, and victims too as we are, but victims of
> a different circumstance, simpler, and therefore, integer for in-
> teger, larger, more heroic and the figures therefore more heroic
> too, not dwarfed and involved but distinct, uncomplex who had
> the gift of loving once or dying once.

Just as Sutpen occupies a detached posture toward his own life as a historical
creature, Mr. Compson distances what he cannot explain; that is, he he-
roicizes his ancestors, thereby severing his blood-and-flesh relationship to
them, as fellow members of a historical community. Thus severed from

his own life, the figures can be manipulated as he wills, and it is not surprising that Mr. Compson conceives of Charles Bon—the sophisticate with whom he most readily identifies—as a "mere spectator" with "the detached attentiveness of a scientist watching the muscles in an anesthetized frog." Bon, he imagines, "took the innocent and negative plate of Henry's provincial soul and intellect and exposed it by slow degrees to this esoteric milieu, building gradually toward the picture which he desired it to retain, accept." Mr. Compson transcendentalizes the "simpler" and "more heroic" figures in a spatialized picture of history as a kind of infinite regress of spectators: "I can see him corrupting Henry," Mr. Compson tells Quentin, describing Bon watching Henry "with that cold and catlike inscrutable calculation, watching the picture resolve and become fixed." Whether the figures in the picture are integers or symbols, in short, the viewer of the picture presumes to stand outside it, and therefore occupies Sutpen's morally impotent posture as the contemplative observer of his own life. Faulkner's condemnation of this posture as embodied in the reader gains force from the way in which he meets—or rather, refuses to meet—our expectations in the novel's final chapter.

As we enter the novel's second movement in chapter 6, we are still waiting, like Bon once was, for the "answer, aware of the jigsaw puzzle integers . . . jumbled and unrecognizable yet on the point of falling into a pattern," the answer which will "reveal . . . at once, like a flash of light," the meaning of the story. As we gradually discover the relation between Bon and Sutpen, and the reason for Sutpen's repudiation of Bon, the events of Sutpen's story begin to compose a coherent picture. But while investing Quentin with the knowledge of Bon's past, Faulkner withholds from us its source, the conversation between Henry and Quentin on that night in September at Sutpen's Hundred. Thus we still don't know "quite all of it," because there is still one thing missing, the verification of Quentin's knowledge about Bon. Accordingly, we await that scene which will allow us to believe what we already know by the time Quentin and Shreve have assembled the story for us, the scene, that is, which will provide proof of Quentin's claim that he learned this crucial fact on that night when he accompanied Rosa to Sutpen's Hundred.

When the confrontation between Quentin and Henry is finally depicted, however, no flash of light comes. Further, this scene not only fails to meet our expectations for verification, but repudiates the very motives for such expectations. The mirror conversation in chapter 9 serves, as it were, to confront us with our own image. It is not only that Faulkner deliberately denies us verification for Quentin's knowledge about Bon; he flaunts that denial, like a rebuke, in our faces. Given this rebuke, the debate about whether we can in fact explain, or whether we are after all not supposed to know, only demonstrates how reified our own consciousness is, for that debate merely traps us between two forms of detached contemplation. It is not that we are not supposed to know, but that we cannot know whether Quentin's statements about Bon are true, and this not because the novel is a paean to the Romantic Imagination, but rather because it is an elegy to it. In other words, if we seek an answer to the question left hanging since the end of chapter 5, the question of what Quentin found out at Sutpen's Hundred, in order to verify the information he seems to have acquired there, we mimic Sutpen in the way Shreve does at the novel's end. We seek to fulfill that need for a final explanation which will account for events by means of a "chemical formula" and this in order to sit back, satisfied with a completed picture from which we can walk away. If, on the other hand, we fall back on imagination to save us, we may avoid playing the detective, but we do not thereby avoid occupying his detached posture, as the case of Mr. Compson abundantly demonstrates. In effect, it is not only Shreve who acts as the reader's surrogate in the novel; it is everyone who speaks, not excluding Sutpen himself. Like Judith, we are responsible, no matter how little we know. Quentin is right when he suspects that "it took . . . Thomas Sutpen to make all of us," because Sutpen's story closes out and gives the lie to the dream of innocence itself, not merely as a literary theme, but as a historical reality. For the boy who was turned away from that "smooth white house" has become, even in Sutpen's eyes, a "boy-symbol," a heroicized figure, now reduced to a ghost who haunts voices "where a more fortunate one would have had a house." Further, those voices speak in the "coffin-smelling gloom" of a "tomb-like room" where men and women cry out in the dark to one another, panting for breath. No novel is more suffused with the virtual smell of death than this one. We may be joined together by that "meager and fragile thread" of speech and hearing which the novel rewinds on its spool, but when Quentin Compson cries out "I dont hate it," the thread has reached its end.

This ending leaves us as readers in an impossible position, for our endeavor to assemble events into an ordered and completed whole has drawn us into the role of participants in the same activity which constitutes the novel's major line of action—narrative construction. Accordingly, when we find our expectations of an ending thwarted by the scene at Sutpen's Hundred, it is for the same reason that, as the dust cloud warns him, Quentin *"will find no destination but will merely abrupt gently onto a plateau and a panorama of harmless and inscrutable night."* For as participants in the same kind of activity which constitutes the stream of event for the participants in the novel's central line of action, we are threatened with becoming, like Quentin, trapped within the very picture we have presumed to compose.

Of course, we insist upon composing that picture, upon resisting that threat. Needless to say, the preceding discussion is itself as much a form of resistance as any other reading of the novel. We cannot avoid resisting the implications of Quentin's position at the novel's end, for the simple reason that the implications are suicidal. What makes our resistance possible, moreover, is also what makes Faulkner's task itself impossible. Printed words cannot become the deeds he struggles to make them here, so that the reader can still treat the book as a spatial object. He can reread or walk away from it, just as if it were a painting on his living room wall. But insofar as Faulkner's strategy succeeds, the reader remains contaminated by his knowledge that, in thus resisting the novel's threat, he is imitating its demonic hero.

Family, Region, and Myth in Faulkner's Fiction

David Minter

Family, region and *myth* are terms that have been prominent in the evaluation and interpretation of Faulkner's fiction for several decades, almost in fact from the beginning. Of all major American writers, Faulkner is the one most clearly associated in our minds with large, extended, elaborately entangled families and with a region, both as actual Mississippi and as imaginary or mythical Yoknapatawpha. Mindful that Faulkner began his life with a strong, even inescapable, sense of family, region, and history; mindful too that he began early to hear and remember stories about his own and other prominent, extended families, as well as stories about his region— about its history and traditions, its victories and defeats, its customs, folkways, mores, and myths; mindful too, that he began early to locate in the stories he was hearing two complementary impulses, one a loyalty to nuance and specificity that rooted stories in local habitations and endowed them with authenticity, the other a revisionary impulse that made room for elaboration and condensation, for displacement and rearrangement; mindful, finally, that Faulkner's own decisive move toward the writing of great fiction coincided and interacted with his imaginative return to family and region as resource and subject—mindful of all these things, many critics have viewed discussion of family, region, and myth in Faulkner's fiction as appropriate, salutary, even inevitable. From this perspective, Faulkner comes to us as our great provincial, not only because he came from our nation's most distinctive province, but also because, in creating his own

From *Faulkner and the Southern Renaissance: Faulkner and Yoknapatawpha, 1981,* edited by Doreen Fowler and Ann J. Abadie. © 1982 by University Press of Mississippi.

elaborate corollary to his inherited province, he raised so many of its particulars to distinctness.

Cleanth Brooks begins *William Faulkner: The Yoknapatawpha Country* with a chapter called "Faulkner the Provincial," and throughout his work he stresses the importance of the sense of community to the fabric of Faulkner's fiction. In an article published in 1974, Joseph Blotner states that "William Faulkner used and transformed more of his own family for his fictional purposes in more books than any other major author" ("The Falkners and the Fictional Families").

Other critics, however, have viewed critical emphasis on Faulkner as a provincial artist with jaundiced eyes, seeing in it yet another instance of the South's vain effort to thumb its nose at the North or, more significantly, as an unfortunate distraction. Near the beginning of a recent review, Sean O'Faolain reiterates the first of these objections, interpreting the statement Faulkner "is our great provincial" as a southern challenge to the northern assumption that "great writing can only thrive on big cities" ("Hate, Greed, Lust and Doom"). Near the end of *Faulkner's Narrative Poetics,* Arthur Kinney states succinctly the second of these points: "European critics and writers have best discerned Faulkner's European roots for a narrative poetics [in symbolist and impressionist literature and art] while we in America have been distracted by southern regionalism, folktale, and myth.

In raising again the question of Faulkner's relation to his region (this paper might well be entitled "Faulkner as Provincial: Yet Again"), and all that relation implied, I intend to assume several things—first, the legitimacy of the issue as established by several decades of critical discourse; second, the advantage of exploring it, as demonstrated by the advances Cleanth Brooks and Joseph Blotner, whom I have quoted, as well as several other critics have made; and third, the partial validity of Kinney's stricture. For Kinney should serve to remind us at least of this: that stress on Faulkner's regionalism need not and should not result in separating his stories from his fictional techniques, a danger Kinney himself seems to me not to have avoided, though his erring in this regard is as it were from the other side. As stories, many of Faulkner's stories strike Kinney as ranging from the "simply unappealing" to the "unattractive and absurd"; for him they are redeemed only by style and form as determined by Faulkner's angle of vision, or as Kinney also puts it, by Faulkner's "narrative poetics." The issues I want to address in this paper are, then, three: whether it is possible at this late date to say anything new about Faulkner's tie to his region; whether, if it is possible to do this, it is possible to do it in a way that helps to explain Faulkner's (and for that matter other southern writers') continuing preoccupation with family and region, history and myth; and third, whether it is possible to do it in a way that helps to clarify the relation between Faulkner's stories as stories, however unappealing, unattractive, and absurd, however pathetic, comic, or heroic they may seem to us, on one side, and his fictional procedures and techniques, however experimental, innovative, and sophisticated they may seem to us, on the other.

In examining these issues, I want, first, to draw on the work of two writers who share several concerns, the most obvious being their concern with America's political history and traditions. In two recent essays Michael Rogin, who teaches political science at the University of California, Berkeley, argues, convincingly I think, that proper understanding of the fiction of Herman Melville depends, among other things, of course, first, on our gauging the importance of Melville's sense of his own family's history as a history of decline; and second, on our discerning in Melville's work a sense, less conscious and therefore less directly articulated, but no less deeply felt, that the history of his own family mirrored the history of the family as an institution, the latter as well as the former being a story of decentering and decline ("Herman Melville: State, Civil Society, and the American 1848").

Although it is impossible for me to do justice to the range and subtlety of Rogin's argument as it pertains to Melville, I do want to suggest some of its pertinence to our understanding of Faulkner. Melville, Rogin's argument runs, felt his family threatened; its status, its power, its very existence seemed to him imperiled. Yet, though he felt this threat with singular force, he did not think of it as singular. Like his cousin Henry Gansevoort, Melville saw his own family fading during an era in which the "family as the unit of government" was also fading: "Today a man is better off without a family at his back. Our Presidents and legislators are selected . . . because they hardly know who were their fathers, our Railroad Kings are foundlings," his cousin wrote (quoted in "The Somers Mutiny and *Billy Budd*: Melville in the Penal Colony"). In an effort to describe the historical context that gave rise to Melville's sense of his fundamental shift, Rogin writes as follows: "By the Gilded Age many [aristocratic] families had disappeared, and with them the family-based order they epitomized. Family was 'the unit of government' and the economy at the [time of the] Revolution; corporation, entrepreneur, politician and party had replaced it a century later." This lost world, Rogin goes on to point out, Melville sought to elegize in varied ways, most transparently in a series of portraits of Major Jack Gentian, the eldest son of two aristocratic descendants of the Revolution and the wearer, by right of "primogeniture," of the "inherited badge of Cincinnati" ("The Somers Mutiny and *Billy Budd*").

In the language of modern social theory, the shift Rogin describes as marking the mind and art of Melville is a shift from a "class society," with its premium on loyalty to family, to a "mass society," with its premium on loyalty to state. Now, as we all have reason to know, Faulkner was not on easy terms with big ideas, social, political, or otherwise.

> Q. "Sir, to what extent were you trying to picture the South and Southern civilization as a whole, rather than just Mississippi—or were you?"
> A. "Not at all. I was trying to talk about people, using the only tool I knew, which was the country that I knew. . . . I don't know anything about ideas, don't have much confidence in them."
>
> *(Faulkner in the University)*

Certainly it is not my intention to make Faulkner sound as though he wrote his fiction mindful of large-scale interpretations of southern history and southern society, let alone the institution of the family. He did not. But he came from a prominent extended family which retained a sense both of its privileged position and of its glamorous history and which saw its own story (or stories) as inseparable from the story (or stories) of its region. In the context from which Faulkner inherited both familial and regional stories, moreover, we can locate a strong political theme as well as a strong aristocratic theme. Writing in 1853, William Gilmore Simms noted that "no periodical can well succeed in the South, which does not include the *political* constituent. The mind of the South is active chiefly in the direction of politics" (quoted in Jay B. Hubbell, *The South in American Literature, 1607–1900*). Looking back a century later, Allen Tate described southern society as "hag-ridden with politics," adding that since "all aristocracies are obsessed politically" their "best intellectual energy goes into politics and goes of necessity" ("The Profession of Letters in the South," *Essays of Four Decades*).

Interpreted broadly, as Simms probably intended and as Tate almost certainly did, *politics* describes as well as any single term can the concerns that dominated the lives of William Faulkner's ancestors, particularly his great-grandfather, the figure who had raised the family to prosperity and prominence. Mississippi, after all, is several hundred miles west of tidewater Virginia, and is a considerably younger society. Its mansions, gardens, and plantations were still new when the Civil War came, and so was its aristocracy. At the time of Faulkner's birth, his family had been prominent for almost as long as North Mississippi had had prominent families, but it had not been prominent very long. As it turned out, moreover, it had become prominent just in time to witness and participate in the disappearance of the Old South as a class- and family-based society and the decline of the family as an institution. Although it is not clear that Faulkner's family as a whole was troubled by a sense of its own and its region's decline, it is certain that his family was aware of the displacement that accompanied what we now know as the rise of the New South, and certain, too, that William Faulkner was troubled both by what was fading and by what was rising. Each of the old aristocratic families that he created—from the Sartorises to the Compsons to the McCaslins—assumes that it is prominent, feels that it is entangled, and senses that it is endangered, and so regards the world around it with alarm.

Faulkner's art was clearly grounded in his knowledge of family and region, or as he put it, in "the country that [he] knew"; and much of what he knew came from stories he had heard—stories his family and region had lived, continued to recount, and by recounting, bequeathed to him. One part of what he gathered from the live traditions around him, beyond, as it were, the stories themselves, was the sensed significances of those stories and the motives imbedded in their telling. With Rogin's work in mind, we can place Faulkner's familial and regional heritage in a context that ties Faulkner's art not only to the work of older writers, such as Melville, or for that matter to Henry Adams, whose three great works elegize the fading of the Middle Ages, the fading of the early Republic, and the fading of the Adams family, but also, as we shall see, to other more recent writers, some southern and some not.

Before expanding this last point, however, I want to turn to another political thinker, one who speaks briefly about Faulkner and his art, and in doing so helps us to understand not so much why Faulkner became absorbed in the history of his family and his region but why he remained absorbed in them and why his absorption took the fictional forms it took. In a footnote to a section of *On Revolution* called "The Revolutionary Tradition and Its Lost Treasure," Hannah Arendt writes as follows: "How such guideposts for future reference and remembrance arise out of this incessant talk, not, to be sure, in the form of concepts but as single brief sentences and condensed aphorisms, may best be seen in the novels of William Faulkner. Faulkner's literary procedure, rather than the content of his work, is highly 'political,' and in spite of many imitations, he has remained, as far as I can see, the only author to use it." I want to come back toward the end of this paper to the issue of whether other writers have used "incessant talk" as Arendt suggests Faulkner used it, but before doing that several things need sorting out, the first being the context in which Arendt links "Faulkner's literary procedure" to "incessant talk."

Arendt's subject, and her regret—that America has lost touch with its revolutionary tradition—need not concern us here. But her sense of how and why that loss occurred should. Her argument runs like this: it is because America has failed "to remember" its revolutionary tradition, and failing "to remember" it has failed to talk of it, or rather to talk of it incessantly, and failing to talk of it incessantly has failed to understand and appropriate it, that it now fears and resists the revolutions of others. For Arendt there is a clear connection between the failure of a people to remember, the failure of a people to talk, and the failure of a people to understand. The gist of her argument together with several of its implications and pertinences emerged clearly in the passage to which her statement about Faulkner is a note. If it is true, she writes, "that all thought begins with remembrance, it is also true that no remembrance remains secure unless it is condensed and distilled" in language. "Experiences and even the stories which grow out of what men do and endure, of happenings and events, sink back into the futility inherent in the living word and the living deed unless they are talked about over and over again. What saves the affairs of mortal men from their inherent futility is nothing but this incessant talk about them, which in its turn remains futile unless . . . certain guideposts for future remembrance, and even for sheer reference, arise out of it." Arendt's position in a passage such as this is obviously tied to a familiar theme in recent intellectual history: to Ernst Cassirer's sense of man as a creature possessing a distinctive symbolic faculty; to Noam Chomsky's sense of man as a creature possessing a distinctive linguistic faculty; and to Roland Barthes's sense of man as a creature possessing a distinctive literary faculty. For Arendt both memory and talking are of critical importance. On our willingness to remember and recount, not knowledge but civilization itself depends, the alternative being not only the loss of living words and living deeds but also a gradual sinking into "ignorance, oblivion." In Arendt's context, no people is without a history but no people possesses its history unless its memory is raised to an active pitch and so becomes articulate, becomes, if we take the word *incessant* seriously, almost compulsively articulate.

Faulkner's fiction, as we all know, is filled with remembering that becomes incessant talking, and I want to turn now to what this implies regarding the nature and motive of Faulkner's imagination, what we might term its "conserving" or "preserving" bent. For Faulkner himself, one factor in the equation was personal: "All that I really desired was a touch-stone simply: a simple word or gesture . . . nothing served but that I try by main strength to recreate between the covers of a book the world as I was already preparing to lose and regret." A part of what Faulkner wanted, we may conclude, was to convey his own sense of his world: to "capture" and "preserve" the "feeling of it." This personal motive is one he shared with many of his characters, including Rosa Coldfield. Among the several things that shock and offend Miss Rosa, one is her awareness that her story, like her life, will soon be lost, that it will most likely never be told in any other way than that in which she is telling it, and that when she is dead, her story as told will be the only story she ever had: "It's because she wants it told," Quentin thinks, early in *Absalom, Absalom!*; "It's because she wants it told."

Finally, however, Miss Rosa's motives are more than personal. In her incessant voice ("Her voice would not cease, it would just vanish"), we sense loyalty that overcomes deep ambivalence. Sitting in an over-tall chair in which she resembles "a crucified child," her "wan haggard face" becomes almost a mask. But as her voice comes and goes, "not ceasing, but vanishing into and then out of the long intervals like a stream," we locate loyalties that, however painfully divided, run deep and touch everything, including family and not-family, region and not-region. All of Miss Rosa's relations— mother, father, sister, niece, nephew, not-husband—are failed relations. In the only town and country she has ever known, she remains curiously at home yet not at home, a native who is also an alien. Finally, however, despite everything, her voice speaks of and for her family, of and for her region: "It's because she wants it told," Quentin says, "so that people whom she will never see" will know at last the story of "the blood of *our* men and the tears of *our* women" (emphasis added).

In *Absalom, Absalom!*, as in the statements of Arendt quoted earlier, remembering and talking have a powerful, even an indispensable social function. On one side, they provide the only adequate means we have of taking possession of the culture we inherit. "How may the Southerner take hold of his Tradition?" Allen Tate once asked. Mindful that the world around him was hostile to the tradition-, family-, class-, and agrarian-based society of the Old South, Tate answers, "by violence"—meaning, as Louis Rubin has noted, a deliberate, aggressive act of will.

In order to be absorbed by individuals, tradition must first be created and possessed by a society; when a society functions properly, moreover, tradition is among the gifts it bequeaths. Violence of the kind that Tate refers to becomes necessary only when a society begins to lose its coherence and force. The world in which Tate found himself—I am referring specifically to his essay called "Remarks on Southern Religion" in *I'll Take My*

Stand—was after all the world in which Faulkner also lived. It was not only a world undergoing rapid change (most worlds seem so to people living through them); nor was it merely a world deeply antagonistic toward the fading culture—the land-, family-, and class-based order—of the Old South; it was also a world almost wholly committed to not remembering. What Arendt implies, Faulkner's fictional strategies establish: that the primary sign of the violence to which Tate refers, its almost inevitable form, is a human voice become more insistent and more incessant.

Although *Absalom, Absalom!* is many things, it is among others a drama of incessant voices in which remembering becomes talking, talking in turn becomes remembering, and remembering, talking. In it we move back from Quentin's beleaguered and divided voice through his father's and Miss Rosa's to Thomas Sutpen's "patient amazed recapitulation." Or, seen another way, we move forward from Miss Rosa's haggard, haunted voice in the first scene to Quentin's still-divided voice in the last. Even the calmest, least insistent of the voices we encounter, Mr. Compson's and Shreve's, speak from and of bafflement, about things that aren't known, that don't add up, that can't finally be taken hold of. Yet, time and again, despite repeated consternation and failure, we see Faulkner's characters moved to remembering and then to talking. Or perhaps it is because of the consternation and failure that they are so moved: "The very disintegration and inadequacy of the world," Lukács once noted, "is the precondition for the existence of art and its becoming conscious" (*The Theory of the Novel; A Historico-Philosophical Essay on the Forms of Great Epic Literature*). The scene with which we begin *Absalom, Absalom!*, an insistent Miss Rosa talking to a reluctant Quentin Compson, is repeated later with Quentin become insistent and Shreve now reluctant. Similarly, the process by which Quentin abandons his reluctance and becomes insistent is later repeated as Shreve moves gradually from a manner and tone that are flippant, even faintly condescending, toward full participation in remembering and recounting. Like Quentin, Shreve moves through a kind of apprenticeship in which listening is the central human act toward moments in which listening gives way to talking. Following an extended collaborative dialogue with Quentin, in chapters 6 and 7, Shreve begins, first, to recall and repeat, and then, slowly to rearrange and elaborate all he had heard and absorbed. As he assimilates and appropriates, he also begins to talk and talk and talk. "No," he says in chapter 7, "you wait. Let me play a while now." In the next chapter, he stands beside a table, wearing an "overcoat buttoned awry . . . look[ing] huge and shapeless like a disheveled bear," and insists on talking until he has gone over everything. Later still he sits with Quentin, as they stare and glare at one another, to go over it again, so that, finally, together, they may move beyond it, at which point listening and talking become so closely allied as to be virtually indistinguishable. "They stared—glared— at one another. It was Shreve speaking, though save for the slight difference . . . inculcated in them (differences not in tone or pitch but of turns of phrase and usage of words), it might have been either of them and was in a sense both: both thinking as one, the voice which happened to be speaking the thought only the thinking become audible, vocal; the two of them creating between them, out of the rag-tag and bob-ends of old tales and talking, people who perhaps had never existed at all anywhere." In the eyes that stare and glare as well as in the voice that insists on doing as it will with what it has been given, the voice that Faulkner first describes and then renders, we observe several things, including a kind of violence that man- ifests itself less obviously in the eyes that glare than in the voice that insists on remembering and talking and playing, on constructing, deconstructing, and reconstructing a long, complex, convoluted story, itself made out of recounting and elaborating on "the rag-tag and bob-ends of old tales and talking." Still, it is not the violence of what Quentin and Shreve do that impresses us so much as the union of mind with mind and of mind with tradition. What Quentin and Shreve come to is not only a kind of creative collaboration; it is also a sense, however fleeting, of atonement, a sense of community.

> "And now," Shreve said, "we're going to talk about love." But he didn't need to say that . . . since neither of them had been thinking about anything else; all that had gone before just so much that had to be overpassed and none else present to overpass it but them. . . . That was why it did not matter to either of them which one did the talking, since it was not the talking alone which did it, performed and accomplished the overpassing, but some happy marriage of speaking and hearing wherein each before the demand, the requirement, forgave con- doned and forgot the faulting of the other—faultings both in the creating of this shade whom they discussed (rather, existed in) and in the hearing and sifting and discarding the false and con- serving what seemed true, or fit the preconceived—in order to overpass to love, where there might be paradox and inconsis- tency but nothing fault nor false.

The unions on which this passage turns include a union between Quentin and Shreve; a union between each of them and the story they tell, as well as the sources and the protagonists of that story; and a union between each of them and not only their story, its protagonists, and its sources, but also the history, the culture, and the traditions that both gave birth to and are captured by that story, its protagonists, and its sources. In addition to being several, these unions are complex, intricate, shifting, and partial. What they share is Faulkner's insistence, first, that each is made possible by a prior union, "some happy marriage between speaking and hearing"; second, that each involves a kind of transcendence, an "overpassing"; and third, that each involves a kind of love—since it is not only love that Quentin and Shreve begin to discuss; it is love they begin to experience.

The sense of community thus created is remarkable on several counts, particularly its inclusivity. For it embraces Quentin and Shreve and the shade and story which they both discuss and exist in; it embraces the other characters who hear and recount and participate in Sutpen's story; and it embraces author and reader alike. Those activities that bring Quentin and Shreve to the happy marriage between speaking and hearing, then to over-passing, and then to love have after all much in common with the habits and activities of mind and spirit that lie behind the making of *Absalom, Absalom!*, just as they have much in common with the habits and activities that any reading of *Absalom, Absalom!* requires. Faulkner is widely thought of as a difficult, uncompromising writer; several readers have felt that he treated most of his characters and all of his readers as Vince Lombardi was said to treat all of his football players, like dogs. There is, of course, some truth in these sentiments. But the other side of Faulkner's demands, the varied difficulties that he strews in our paths, is a remarkable generosity. No writer has shared more fully the tasks and even the prerogatives of the writer with his characters, and none has shared them more fully with his readers. In the listening and talking in which Quentin and Shreve engage—their remembering and sorting and recounting, even more their creative extensions of the rag-tag and bob-ends given them—we locate primitive versions of Faulkner's larger labor; in their willingness to listen and listen and listen, to try, as it were, for total recall, in their willingness to arrange and rearrange, to remember and surmise and speculate, to work and play endlessly, we locate models of many things required of us as readers.

Like them, furthermore, we come curiously to view all knowing as re-knowing, all cognition as re-cognition, even as we come to view all knowledge and cognition as tentative, provisional, imperfect. "Really, uni-versally," Henry James once remarked, "relations stop nowhere, and the exquisite problem of the artist is eternally but to draw, by a geometry of his own, the circle within which they shall happily *appear* to do so" (Preface to *Roderick Hudson*). No such geometry exists for Faulkner's characters, nor even in James's triumphant terms, for Faulkner himself. His novels—at least his Yoknapatawpha stories, clearly the heart of his achievement—reach beyond themselves to one another. They give us the sense of beginnings, the sense of endings. We know without being told that Miss Rosa's talking and Quentin's listening have been going on a long time before we too begin to listen and talk. On the last page of the novel, Quentin's voice, with its curious blend of affirmation and denial, vanishes without ceasing. In between we come repeatedly to moments of illumination in which we at least feel ourselves on the verge of seeing everything clearly, only to discover again our bafflement.

> "You cant understand it," [Quentin says to Shreve]. "You would have to be born there."
> "Would I then?" Quentin did not answer. "Do you understand it?"
> "I don't know," Quentin said. "Yes, of course I understand it." They breathed in the darkness. After a moment Quentin said: "I dont know."

Of Quentin's and Shreve's inventions, on which so much of the novel depends, we know that they are "probably true enough," but we also know that they involve people and events that "perhaps had never existed at all anywhere." From beginning to end, the mood of the novel is interrogative and tentative.

> Maybe we are both Father. Maybe nothing ever happens once and is finished. Maybe happen is never once but like ripples maybe on water after the pebble sinks . . . Yes, we are both Father. Or maybe Father and I are both Shreve, maybe it took Father and me both to make Shreve or Shreve and me both to make Father or maybe Thomas Sutpen to make all of us.
>
> (Italics omitted)

A few years earlier, around 1931, Faulkner had played with related contingencies wondering whether he had created the world of his fiction with its "shady but ingenious shapes" or "it had invented me." Given such fundamental contingencies, tentativenesses that touch everything, Faulkner's characters are doomed to circle almost endlessly. "Wait, I tell you!" Quentin says to Shreve; and then to himself: "Am I going to have to have to hear it all again . . . I am going to have to hear it all over again I am already hearing it all over again I am listening to it all over again I shall have to never listen to anything else but this again forever." Yet, even as everything Quentin and Shreve learn remains tentative, hedged here with statements that seem to balance and cancel one another, or there with a long string of maybes, it also comes to us as something already known. For Quentin in particular everything heard or seen, including those things we have heard him hear or say or seen him see, come to him always as both strange and familiar, new and old.

> But you were not listening, because you knew it all already, had learned, absorbed it already without the medium of speech somehow from having been born and living beside it, with it, as children will and do: so that what your father was saying did not tell you anything so much as it struck, word by word, the resonant strings of remembering. You had been here before, seen those graves more than once . . . just as you had seen the old house too, been familiar with how it would look before you even saw it . . . No, you were not listening; you didn't have to.

Quentin listens, of course, listens even when he does not appear to be listening, even when weariness and reluctance well up in him. He has grown up with more stories than we will ever know, with names "interchangeable and almost myriad." His "very body," we read early, "was an empty hall echoing with sonorous defeated names; he was not a being, an entity, he was a commonwealth." For him all knowing begins with remembering and depends upon talking. The stories that come to him, word by word, to strike "the resonant strings of remembering," provide the only access he has to his cultural heritage; the stories he hears, tells, and seeks to finish are the only means he has of absorbing, appropriating, assimilating his culture. In addition, they are the only means he has of moving beyond both the dangerous desires and the harsh judgments that memory and knowledge arouse within him. Although the stories he hears complicate everything for him, provoking contradictory desires and judgments, they provide his only hope of mastery and his only hope of peace. What this suggests proves in fact to be of crucial importance, for the stories that come to Quentin word by word to strike "the resonant strings of remembering," also create the only avenue he has for exploring the depths of his own consciousness. In Faulkner's fiction remembering serves a personal function in addition to the socially indispensable function Arendt helps us to locate. What is curious, if not striking, about this, however, is the loose analogy Faulkner seems to establish between the social and the personal, between our explorations of culture and our explorations of consciousness. Like our access to culture, our access to consciousness, at least so far as Quentin is concerned, turns on our willingness to remember, our willingness to talk incessantly, even our willingness to listen interminably. In *Absalom, Absalom!*, the shadowy past toward which remembering, listening, and talking take us is always double; although it forever remains just beyond our reach, it holds the secrets of our people and the secrets of our selves. Such glimpses as we gain, within and beyond us, are always of things remembered and discovered, familiar and strange, old and new, and they always come as sights desired and pursued, dreaded and shunned, and therefore as things held, if at all, tenuously. On both the cultural and personal levels, moreover, such seeing, if it is to become knowing, must be in part a matter of absorbing and in part a matter of constructing. *Knowing* may begin with copying, but as Piaget has suggested, it always involves acting: "It means constructing systems of transformations. . . . Knowing reality means constructing systems of transformations that correspond, more or less adequately, to reality. Knowledge, then, is a system of transformations that become progressively adequate (*Genetic Epistemology*).

Viewed from such a perspective, *Absalom, Absalom!* remains, whatever else it is, a drama of incessant voices: a drama in which the human acts of remembering, talking, and listening become "interchangeable and almost myriad"; a drama in which these acts provide man's only means of taking hold of the experiences and traditions that have shaped his family and his region, as well as his only means of exploring his own consciousness; and a drama in which these acts, given the stakes they entail, must under proper force prove as dangerous as they are necessary. In addition, however, *Absalom, Absalom!* becomes a model, a trying out, of what *knowing* in its fullest sense actually means. Knowing in *Absalom, Absalom!* begins with remembering, talking, and listening; and it involves considerable *copying* in the form of repetition, not only of countless details and events but even of voices: to Quentin, Shreve "sounds just like father," and for the reader the several voices of the novel seem to merge into a resonant medley charged with echoes. But *knowing* moves in the novel toward transformations— toward arrangements and re-arrangements, toward inventions and creations. What Quentin and Shreve do overtly, even boldly—which is to transform the givens they receive—other characters in the novel do covertly or timidly. *Absalom, Absalom!* traces, then, a series "of transformations that correspond, more or less adequately," to its givens, its reality; and though knowing, for its characters and readers alike, remains tentative and imperfect, unfolding and unfinished, the series "of transformations" it traces do "become progressively adequate."

My long look at *Absalom, Absalom!* notwithstanding, it is my intention in this paper to make suggestions pertinent both to the larger reaches of Faulkner's Yoknapatawpha fiction and to the writings of other southern writers. As a move in that direction, I want to invoke a term from my title that I have thus far almost wholly ignored. In his foreword to *Brother to Dragons,* Robert Penn Warren remarks that "historical sense and poetic sense should not, in the end, be contradictory, for if poetry is the little myth we make, history is the big myth we live, and in our living, constantly remake." History or the past is, as we know, never dead in Faulkner's fiction, and sometimes it is not even past; his characters are often preoccupied or obsessed with the past, and even when they are not, they and their worlds are shaped by it. Still, Faulkner is not in the usual sense of the term an historical novelist. His sense of the past is neither nostalgic nor sentimental, which means that his art is dedicated neither to recapturing the past as it was nor to investing or charging it with the emotions of the present. In the remembering and talking and listening, in the assimilations and the transformations that take place in *Absalom, Absalom!,* the explorations of history and the creation of myth occur simultaneously. Although one part of the process is "the hearing and sifting and discarding" of what seems false, and another part the hearing "and conserving" of what seems true, neither the one nor the other separates history from myth. For another part of the process, somehow beyond yet continuous with the discarding of what seems false and the conserving of what seems true, but no less important and no less legitimate, is the game of transformation: the game of inventing and creating people and events that seem right, people and events that are "probably true enough" even though they perhaps never "existed at all anywhere," or more radically, even if they never existed. In this context, man makes myth as he explores history.

Another part of the figure I am trying to describe here can, I think, be got at by recalling an observation of W. B. Yeats, that it is of our quarrel with society that we make rhetoric and of our quarrel with ourselves that we make poetry. If for Faulkner we may say that it is of our quarrel and struggle with our traditions, our culture, that we make myth, and of our quarrel with ourselves that we make poetry, we no doubt simplify too much, leave too much out. But we gain this at least: a clear sense of how inseparable the two parts of this process were for him, and a clear sense of why he made every instance of one at some level a version of the other. Remembering, talking, listening, as activities and as terms, get mixed up in Faulkner's fiction in a thousand ways. Finally, however, there is a seamlessness to them, just as there is a seamlessness to the stories they yield, to the form those stories take, and to the hedged and tentative knowledge they bequeath. Every exploration of family becomes an exploration of region, and every exploration of either becomes an exploration of self. If we distinguish myth from poetry, allying "myth" with culture and history, and allying "poetry" with consciousness and self, we do so in the name of convenience, knowing that in *Absalom, Absalom!* myth and poetry alike, the hold we have on culture and the hold we have on self come from stories that in turn come from remembering and talking and listening incessantly.

"What shall we say who have knowledge carried to the heart?" asks the protagonist of Allen Tate's "Ode to the Confederate Dead," in a line that puts as succinctly as any I know the question Faulkner's characters and readers alike face repeatedly. Some such question also lies behind books as different as *All the King's Men* and *North toward Home,* as well as Tate's "Ode" and much of Warren's recent fine poetry. In *I'll Take My Stand,* to take a very different case, a book of essays whose reputation continues to rise and fall, remembering, talking, and knowing, if not seamless activities, are at least closely allied, as are history, myth, and poetry. The form of *I'll Take My Stand,* its motives and procedures, may well be of more historical, or in Arendt's terms of more "political," significance than its explicit themes, as they are certainly of more aesthetic significance. Arendt suggests that Faulkner alone, despite "many imitations," has succeeded in turning "incessant talking" into art. But Faulkner's career coincided, from the mid to late twenties into the thirties and beyond, with the remarkable flowering of Southern writing that we now call the Southern Renaissance, and like the years of his life, the concerns that manifest themselves in his art were shared. Those concerns touched family, region, and the past as they impinge upon consciousness, but they also touched his sense that knowing begins with remembering, follows talking and listening, and ends in transformations. Tradition, to borrow Tate's inclusive term, is important, then, not because it is fixed and finished but rather because it is not; nor, to paraphrase Marianne Moore's description of poetry, "because a / high-sounding interpretation can be put upon" it, but rather because, given its fluidity and incompleteness, it invites play as well as loyalty and so enables poets to present "for inspection, imaginary gardens with real toads in them," which may be as close as poets come to offering us "guideposts for future remembrance, and even for sheer reference" ("Poetry").

*A*bsalom, Absalom! and the House Divided

Eric J. Sundquist

As [Faulkner] turned from *Light in August* to *Absalom, Absalom!* (1936) he turned from the tragedy of Jim Crow to the tragedy that made him possible—indeed, it seems, inevitable—and he did so by turning . . . to the sins of the fathers that led necessarily to the violence of the brothers. He brings to a culmination, with an intensity only the war and its aftermath could make visible, the several fratricidal dimensions of America's national sin; and his novel ends . . . in forged reunion and escape from the darkest past of the South. It ends in 1909 in an old abolitionist stronghold in New England, having precariously reunited its story to the unfulfilled vision of *The Sound and the Fury* by leading Quentin Compson through an agonizing rehearsal of Thomas Sutpen's flawed design, through the *might have been* that had to be, and bringing him to the threshold of his suicide.

The flaw in Thomas Sutpen's grand "design" is, of course, his first son's supposed black blood. Abandoning his wife and son in Haiti, Sutpen carries his dynastic scheme to frontier Mississippi, only to have that repressed son return as his second son's best friend and apparently, his daughter's fiancé. Sutpen does not (according to Quentin, according to his father, according to his grandfather) call it "retribution, no sins of the fathers come home to roost," but just a "mistake," one that inescapably impedes his vision of "fine grandsons and great-grandsons springing as far as the eye could reach" and leaves him immobilized in attempting to fathom its meaning. He can either recognize Charles Bon or not recognize him, he says, "either destroy my design with my own hand" or, letting the affair take

From *Faulkner: The House Divided*. © 1983 by the Johns Hopkins University Press.

its own course, "see my design complete itself quite normally and naturally and successfully to the public eye, yet to my own in such a fashion as to be a mockery and a betrayal." This re-creation of Sutpen's dilemma by Quentin and Shreve occurs at a significant point in the "design" both of Faulkner's book and his career that we must consider; we must consider as well the question of whether or not Sutpen is a representative southern planter, a point of some critical debate. That debate, however, is not nec-essarily relevant to the issue of miscegenation. The average planter did not rise from tidewater poverty, conceive a grand design in answer to being turned away from the front door of a plantation by a "monkey nigger," sail to Haiti and participate in an ongoing racial revolution, and see his dreams of grandeur shattered when his white son murders the "black" brother who is going to marry his sister. Still, the contours of Sutpen's mythic career are certainly more accurately revealing than the equally mythic magnolia-scented portraits by Thomas Nelson Page, Thomas Dixon, and Margaret Mitchell, which enjoyed, in complete contrast, such extraordinary popularity in Jim Crow's South. It is the context of such rampantly nostalgic versions of slavery that Faulkner's novel becomes most powerful and Sutpen's resolute "innocence" most meaningful. For that "innocence"—the last barrier to Sutpen's tragic recognition and the last threat holding Faulkner's lost dream in place—is the strangling center of southern nostalgia. Without it, even the remembered design falls into ruins.

There is no way to overestimate the stupendous, tortuous effort Faulk-ner makes in *Absalom, Absalom!* to force into crisis and overcome the tragic divisions his novel is built upon; the repeated metaphor of that effort, and its perfect formal analogy, is marriage and its implied recognitions and responsibilities. It operates throughout the book in ways we must account for, but it derives its power quite simply from expressing, at its deepest, potentially most tragic and threatening level, one central issue that the Civil War would in retrospect seem to be about and the issue *Absalom, Absalom!* is so outrageously about: amalgamation—or rather, miscegenation. It is worth making this distinction, for *miscegenation* first came into being as a term in 1863, almost on the heels of the Emancipation Proclamation. *Amal-gamation* meant simply a mixing, but *miscegenation* quite clearly meant in-terracial *sexual* mixing, and the term therefore quickly acquired a contagious and derisive force, one that expressed the nation's most visceral fears, par-adoxical or not, about emancipation.

. . . Lincoln's 1857 defense against charges that the Republican party encouraged miscegenation took the logical form of pointing out that his not wishing to own a black woman did not entail his wishing to marry one. Clearly, miscegenation was not the only point of conflict between the sections, and the charges against Lincoln were not taken overly seriously by anyone in the North; indeed, they largely subsided until emancipation became probable and, finally, actual. In late December 1863, they exploded again in the form of an anonymous pamphlet entitled "Miscegenation: The Theory of the Blending of the Races, Applied to the American White Man and Negro." The proslavery authors coined the term *miscegenation* (from *miscere,* to mix, and *genus,* race) and represented the pamphlet as the work of an abolitionist, in hopes of discrediting the Republican party in the upcoming elections. Only miscegenation, the pamphlet claimed, could insure the progress and prosperity of the country; the war would guarantee not only physical freedom for blacks but also sexual freedom for both races, particularly in the South, where organized interracial breeding would be carried out on a massive scale and white women would at last be free to give expression to their secret passions. Eventually the pamphlet was recognized as a hoax, but not before it unleashed a barrage of attacks and a strong response from J. H. Van Evrie, whose "Subjenation: The Theory of the Normal Relation of the Races" exactly imitated the style and format of "Miscegenation" but argued violently against its doctrines. As the 1864 campaign progressed, the charges against the Republicans and Lincoln grew more hysterical. One pamphleteer claimed, for example, that the Republicans were plotting to kill or castrate all southern white men and apportion their women for the use of "Black Ourang-Outangs." Others spoke of Lincoln's "Miscegenation Proclamation" or depicted him in political cartoons and prints as the sponsor of miscegenation, while one leaflet offered a "Black Republican Prayer," which parodied the Lord's Prayer and called upon "the spirit of amalgamation" to shine forth and flourish, "that we may become a regenerated nation of half-breeds, and mongrels" and "live in bonds of fraternal love, union, and equality with the Almighty Nigger, henceforward, now and forever. Amen."

Such charges, again, were not taken seriously by a very large number of people in the North; but they became widely, if not universally, credible in the South—if only at a profound emotional and rhetorical level. In the case of Van Evrie, the refutation of the ameliorating theory of miscegenation was a passion; he had already written *Negroes and Negro "Slavery"* (1861), and, when the book was reissued in 1868 as *White Supremacy and Negro Subordination,* its claims seemed more vehement and relevant than ever. It has to be noted, however, that since Van Evrie argued against *all* miscegenation, throughout the world and in the slaveholding South, as well as against what he thought to be the most serious menace posed by emancipation, he is in important respects emblematic of the schizophrenic position of the South in particular and the nation in general. In the "awful perversion of the instincts of reproduction" that we see around us daily in the South, Van Evrie wrote, God's design is transformed into "the most loathsome and most hideous of social miseries." Abolition will only further this degeneration; once it is accomplished, we will be left for years "to struggle with the load of sin and disease thus brought upon ourselves by our crimes against reason and the ordinances of the Eternal," and will require a span of time that "cannot be estimated with any certainty" in order finally "to recover from the foul and horrible contamination of admixture with the blood of the negro." Like his Jim Crow counterpart, Charles Carroll, Van Evrie held mulattoes responsible for nearly all crimes and racial disorder, and he attacked the "strange and disgusting delusion," the "diseased sentimentality" of the North, which casts "an air of romance" over mongrel women while the terrible miseries of "their own white sisters falling every hour from the ranks of pure womanhood" are totally disregarded.

Because he anticipated, among other things, the hysterical defense of southern womanhood that would become and remain the touchstone of white racism, it is no wonder that Van Evrie's book seemed more to the point after the war than it had upon initial publication. That anticipation is significant, however, for it serves to enact the mechanism of repression that the war revealed—a mechanism that had certainly been at work in the antebellum South all along but became necessarily more and more extravagant in its aftermath. Such repression inevitably entangled an outcry against threatened sexual violence by blacks and a vehement denial of similar violence by whites (or, if not its denial, its fanatically righteous justification), a denial that Van Evrie's own protests could not reduce and one, as we will see, that took a logical and tragic form, Even *Gone with the Wind* (1936), that rarified epic fantasia of the Jim Crow South, would manage to suggest that the many "ignominies and dangers" brought upon the South by Reconstruction "were as nothing compared with the peril of white women." Such a particular fear amid a more general anarchy leads Scarlett O'Hara to feel for the first time "a kinship with the people around her." Because it held the invading Yankees most responsible for miscegenation in the South, Mitchell's novel of hot-blooded gynealotry and patriotic fervor could, of course, make little allusion to the requisite counterpoint of this hysteria, the absolute perversion of "kinship" that Mary Chesnut recorded in her notorious diary entry of 1861:

We live surrounded by prostitutes. An abandoned woman is sent out of any decent house elsewhere. Who thinks any worse of a negro or a mulatto woman for being a thing we can't name? God forgive us, but ours is a *monstrous* system and wrong and iniquity. Perhaps the rest of the world is as bad—this *only* I see. Like the patriarchs of old our men live all in one house with their wives and their concubines, and the mulattoes one sees in every family exactly resemble the white children—and every lady tells you who is the father of all the mulatto children in everybody's household, but those in her own she seems to think drop from the clouds, or pretends to think so.

(*Mary Chesnut's Civil War*, C. Vann Woodward, ed.)

Chestnut might certainly have endorsed Van Evrie's contention that "*mulattoism is to the South what prostitution is to the North*," but she could have agreed only in figurative terms with his insistence that, just as in cases of prostitution and incest, so in the case of mulattoism Nature opposes this "monstrous violation of the physical integrity of the races," this " 'original sin,' as it may well be termed," by physiologically punishing the children it produces "to the third and fourth generations for the sins of the fathers" (*White Supremacy and Negro Subordination*).

Van Evrie's theory of degeneration depended on detecting a "similarity of species" between the *mulatto* and the *mule* (they have the same etymology), one that results in a "diminishing vitality," a "tendency to disease and disorganization," and an eventual sterility among the "mongrel" element, and therefore insures that it will never be "of sufficient amount to threaten the safety or even disturb the peace of Southern society." This rather striking conclusion is only unsurprising when it is recognized to contain (or sublimate) one threat by dismissing another. When the book was first published before the war, the theory of degeneration (with its biblical sanction of punishment unto the fourth generation) was a scathing critique of slaveholding miscegenation; after the war, it could only appear to express as well an ironic rationalization of the counter-threat abolition seemed to entail. Van Evrie was not whistling in the dark, however, for at a social and psychological level the punishment of the third and fourth generations (of all generations) was real indeed—so real that Faulkner himself would seek recourse in the figure of physiological degeneration in order to describe the dilemma of Jim Bond, the fourth-generation descendant in *Absalom, Absalom!* of his family's "original sin," whose unintelligible howling unites the novel's disparate voices and engulfs their frantic attempts to salvage the Sutpen dynasty in a single anguished cry. As Shreve says to Quentin Compson on the last page of the book, there is still "one nigger Sutpen left. Of course you can't catch him and you don't even always see him and you never will be able to use him. But you've got him there still."

This is the conclusion of the novel, however, and to reach it Faulkner had first to create a design and, it seems, to destroy it with his own hand. To see clearly how he did so, we must see clearly how central the facts and metaphors of marriage are in *Absalom, Absalom!* Van Evrie was certainly not alone in thinking that marriage among slaves, because they are governed by "capricious affections" and characterized by a "feeble moral nature," would be "obviously unnatural, monstrous, and wicked." By situating his observations on this subject within the context of a romantic tribute to the sacred institution of white marriage, Van Evrie once more made painfully explicit the reason why miscegenation was the gravest threat to slavery in the South (and would seem the even graver result of abolition). It made a mockery of white marriage in a particular and terrifying way—by making the races indistinguishable (in theory and sometimes eventually in fact) and by making them, therefore, *equal*. The South was destroying its own design by sinning against God's design. The precarious balance between these points of view—between slavery itself as sin and miscegenation alone as sin—is one that would drive both the South and the nation into fantastic forms of refutation and denial for the next hundred years, forms as utterly deranged and precious (and immensely popular) as *Gone with the Wind,* and as penetrating and tragic (and widely ignored) as *Absalom, Absalom!*

That these two books—both obsessed with marriage and family to the point of obscuring the political crisis of civil war to which they refer—could appear in the same year at first seems almost irrational. Mitchell's novel, of course, sold millions of copies and became America's favorite movie; Faulkner's novel was greeted with perplexity, disbelief, and outrage. The one made clear to some observers how strange Jim Crow's career was, while the other measured the length and complexity of that career by exposing the enervating intimacies within the grand design that made it possible. Both in their complementary ways continued to measure the physical and emotional entanglements between white and black in the South, the one by denying the sins of the fathers altogether, the other by expressing their intimate, intolerable actuality. Yet it is only when we see how much of *Gone with the Wind* Faulkner had, as it were, internalized in *Absalom, Absalom!* that its full significance is made clear. Scarlett O'Hara descends not only (ironically enough) from Stowe's Nina Gordon and from countless white heroines in the novels of Dixon, Page, and others, but she is also much the antecedent of the sister Quentin Compson could never truly possess, the one Faulkner could never clearly portray. The one impossible marriage *Absalom, Absalom!* refers to continually is the one that divides the house of Compson and the house of Sutpen alike, brings the two into momentary union before tearing them apart, and creates the extraordinary psychological and stylistic turbulence in Faulkner's reimagining of Quentin's dilemma. It also, we shall see, raise from the detritus of eccentric observation to the dignity of acute psychological truth a passage from Mississippian Henry Hughes's *Treatise on Sociology* (1854), whose seeming burlesque of syllogistic argument is a perfect index of the tormenting issue of miscegenation:

> Hybridism is heinous. Impurity of races is against the law of nature. Mulattoes are monsters. The law of nature is the law of God. The same law which forbids consanguinous amalgamation forbids ethnical amalgamation. Both are incestuous. Amalgamation is incest.

Although it obviously played no part in Faulkner's writing of *Absalom, Absalom!* and though he amusingly claimed in 1937 that he had not read it because it was "entirely too long for any story," *Gone with the Wind* provides an interesting emotional context for Faulkner's novel insofar as it represents the version of the Civil War Faulkner claimed he got from "the maiden spinster aunts which had never surrendered." One of them, Faulkner reported in 1958, went to see the film version, "and as soon as Sherman came on the screen she got up and left." Miss Rosa Coldfield might have done just that. While she does not finally dominate the novel, Rosa's obsessive rehearsals for Quentin of Sutpen's failed dynasty, the murder of Bon, and her own tortured courtship by the "ogre" generate the atmosphere of spent dreams and feverishly maintained innocence in and against which subsequent versions of the tragedy are played out. The novel's magnificent opening scene between Rosa and Quentin is itself a kind of courtship, a ritual immersion of Quentin into the gothic convulsions of Rosa's fading by hyperdistilled erotic memories. The turning rhythms of Faulkner's prose here, as elsewhere, create a strained communion in which Quentin and Rosa, breathing and memory, body and house and voice, are fused in a sensation of calm that is poised nevertheless on the extreme edge of violence.

The extraordinary balance between nostalgia and rage, in which the solid present—the dust, the screens, the heated air, the twice-bloomed wisteria—breaks down into the resurrected ghost of past grandeur, the stillborn lust of Rosa's "impotent yet indomitable frustration," creates an eroticism not simply of the flesh but of memory—creates of Rosa herself the demon she accuses Sutpen of being and (as Mr. Compson later expresses it) an "instrument of retribution" rising "bloodless and without dimension from the sacrificial stone of the marriage-bed." The exact purpose of that retribution is made no clearer to us than Rosa is able to make it to herself; and it is not clearly retribution at all, for as she tells Quentin of Sutpen's proposal that they breed on trial before getting married, "*I forgave him. . . . Why shouldn't I? I had nothing to forgive.*" Rosa's balked courtship and marriage to Sutpen do, as Shreve will suggest, leave her "irrevocably husbanded" to an "abstract carcass of outrage and revenge"—but not in her version of the courtship, which is less a smoldering desire for revenge than an excessively melodramatic lament over the denial of desire itself. Rosa is neither wife nor mother; in one respect she is for Faulkner emblematic of those war widows who were never brides at all, the many undefeated for whom the war took not only their land, their slaves, their golden dream but also the men they would never have. And in the nervously exposed contours of her passion Rosa also betrays, as the novel restrains her sister, Ellen, and her niece, Judith, from doing, a further aspect of the crisis of union the war would release into the hysteria of racism for a century to come.

Rosa's "demonizing," as nearly every reader of *Absalom, Absalom!* has characterized it, is certainly conspicuous, but it only becomes significant when it is seen within the context of her now brittle but still tender passion and grief for her first "nothusband," "*Charles Bon, Charles Good, Charles Husband-soon-to-be.*" The "*shadow-realm of make-believe*" in which her passion lives, the "*fairy-tale*" she creates for herself and the young man she never sees, even in death, brings Rosa closer to incest than her later courtship by Sutpen will, and it brings her close to an act of miscegenation she does not recognize as such. Or so it seems. There is no direct evidence in the novel that Rosa ever knows Bon is a "Negro," but then there is no direct evidence that Quentin does either, and his peculiar testimony is assumed to be conclusive, at least to the extent that nearly all readers of the novel take it for granted. He finds out the truth about Bon when he visits Sutpen's Hundred with Rosa—not, apparently, from Henry but from Clytie. As Shreve puts it, "She didn't tell you in so many words because she was still keeping that secret for the sake of the man who had been her father too . . . she didn't tell you, it just came out of the terror and the fear after she turned you loose and caught the Aunt Rosa's arm and the Aunt Rosa turned and struck her hand away."

The 1909 scene repeats the 1865 scene Rosa has already described to

Quentin, in which Clytie attempts to stop her from mounting the stairs to Judith's room after Bon is murdered. It is worth reproducing a portion of this scene, for it is the heart of Rosa's chapter and brings into focus the conflicting passions and stunned recognitions of consanguinity that compel the entire novel. Approaching the stairs to see at last the dead Bon she would never see, Rosa is stopped first by the *"immobile antagonism"* of Clytie's face, by her body, which seems to *"project upward something . . . inherited from an older and a purer race than mine"* and shapes in the air between them *"that bedroom long-closed and musty, that sheetless bed"* and its *"pale and bloody corpse."* When her commands to Rosa fail to stop her, Clytie grasps her arm:

> *Then she touched me, and then I did stop dead. . . . my entire being seemed to run at blind full tilt into something monstrous and immobile, with a shocking impact too soon and too quick to be mere amazement and outrage at that black arresting and untimorous hand on my white woman's flesh. Because there is something in the touch of flesh with flesh which abrogates, cuts sharp and straight across the devious intricate channels of decorous ordering, which enemies as well as lovers know because it makes them both. . . . We just stood there—I motionless in the attitude and action of running, she rigid in that furious immobility, the two of us joined by that hand and arm which held us, like a fierce rigid umbilical cord, twin sistered to the fell darkness which had produced her. . . . And then suddenly it was not outrage that I waited for, out of which I had instinctively cried; it was not terror: it was some cumulative over-reach of despair itself. . . . I cried—perhaps not aloud, not with words (and not to Judith, mind: perhaps I knew already, on the instant I entered the house and saw that face which was at once both more and less than Sutpen, perhaps I knew even then what I could not, would not, must not believe)—I cried "And you too? And you too, sister, sister?"*

Like so many passages in the novel, this one (if not at first, certainly in retrospect) intimates the secret of Bon's blood, but it does so in a fashion charged with ambiguous power. Rosa's shocked exclamation, "you too, sister, sister?" suggests not only that Clytie is clearly Judith's sister (Sutpen's daughter), and not only that Clytie, like Rosa, may be vicariously in love with Bon, but also that those possibilities reveal two further ones that constitute, in Faulkner's imagination if not her own, precisely what Rosa "could not, would not, must not believe" and what the novel holds in passionate suspense: that Bon is Clytie's "brother" and that Bon is "black."

The scene does not spell out this recognition, but it certainly suggests it more pointedly than does Quentin's climactic visit to Sutpen's Hundred forty-five years later. When the three of them—Rosa, Judith, and Clytie, "*as though we were one being, interchangeable*"—await Sutpen's return after the war, Rosa speaks of Clytie as one who embodies of the war's "*perverse and inscrutable paradox: free, yet incapable of freedom who had never once called herself a slave*" and, moreover, "*who in the very pigmentation of her flesh represented that debacle which had brought Judith and me to what we were.*" In between this assertion of Clytie's tragedy and the earlier scene that so clarifies the "debacle" she represents, Rosa speaks passionately, with the rapture of fantasized violation and husbanding, of the "*world filled with living marriage*" that only imagination can create.

Rosa's failed courtships, one in imagination and one in fact, have often and quite rightly been read as the rhetorical highpoints of Faulkner's novel; but the psychological complexities of her expressed passion—complexities that the novel both reveals and buries at the same time—have for good reason resisted elaboration. In particular, the issue of miscegenation has been largely ignored because it is assumed that Rosa suspects nothing of Bon's parentage. Because it is the strategy of *Absalom, Absalom!* to intimate but suppress its critical information until the very end, and even then to reveal it only in the dramatic, self-reflexive mask of tacit recognition, however, the true torment of Rosa's courtship by Sutpen may only be explicable if we assume—as the scene between Rosa and Clytie suggests—that Rosa herself, perhaps vicariously, understands the full dimensions of Bon's tragedy as well as Sutpen's. The "debacle" represented by Clytie's "pigmentation" is purposely ambiguous: it is the debacle of slavery and the war itself that makes Judith and Rosa widows without having been brides; but it is also the debacle of miscegenation, which the novel so continually engages as the curse and sin that brings Sutpen's design, like that of the South itself, to collapse. It is the debacle that makes Clytie neither slave nor free (neither before nor after the war) and makes Charles Bon neither slave nor son and brother. Like the motive for Bon's murder, the psychological tragedy Rosa's failed dream represents must be seen to exist in the interstices of the novel's action and its assumptions about the crisis of consanguinity; for if it seems to gather together and swallow up the grief Ellen and Judith never express, and therefore to transfer into the atmosphere of volatile fantasy the one passion in actuality Faulkner seems unable or unwilling to articulate, it does so with a particular emotional urgency.

Although the language of Rosa's re-created courtship, its burgeoning moment of passion held forever on the brink of fulfillment, contains as clear an expression of the recognized truth about Bon as we may wish, there is no reason to insist on its actuality. What matters, rather, is that Faulkner, in creating this powerful scene, should invest so much deliberate energy in drawing the fated Bon toward recognition at all, a recognition the novel intimates again and again but that its events can actualize only in brutal denial. What else does Bon want but recognition—by his sister, his brother, his father? And why should not Rosa, the fever of her vicarious life driving her toward that recognition, see now in Clytie's darkened face what we are to imagine Quentin sees half a century later? Faulkner does not present that recognition clearly in either instance; his language is thoroughly charged with it, however, charged with a recognition wasted and betrayed year after year, beyond Quentin's death and well into Faulkner's life, but charged as well, Rosa's ecstatic memories tell us, with a recognition more vital and lasting—and threatening—than we may wish. In this book filled with shadows blurring into visions, with unliving marriage and passion consummated in death, it is entirely appropriate that this scene bring us to the verge of a recognition we are unwilling to make, that it vitalize the scene, the act, the moment that never *will be* in the certain tragic fullness of what *might have been*.

Southern gynealotry and, in this instance, the fanatic undefeat of the maidens and spinsters whose "nothusbands" never came home, include and themselves express an acute psychological division that makes dramatically immediate the other forms of divided sensibility *Absalom, Absalom!* explores. The "monstrous" antagonism that Rosa confronts in the form of Clytie is nothing less than that which Mary Chestnut found "monstrous" about slavery—its sexual crimes, not simply their physical violence but even more so, perhaps, the emotional violence that miscegenation entailed. That violence enclosed both black and white, parents and children, husbands and wives in a cage of paradoxical feelings. To the extent that "sexual intimacy strikingly symbolized a union he wished to avoid," Winthrop Jordan writes, the slaveholder could indeed deny the fruits of his passion by not recognizing them. Because they confused the essential distinction between the races, mulattoes threatened to "undermine the logic of the racial slavery upon which his society was based," and by classifying them as Negroes, the slaveholder-father "was in effect denying that intermixture had occurred at all." But that inevitably put his wife, and southern white women in general, in a peculiar position, for it heightened the mythic melodrama of gallantry and courtesy that almost every account, fictional or not, makes characteristic of the slaveholding South. The confusing atmosphere in which the white woman was asked to live, Jordan remarks, "warped her affective life in two directions at once." As she was made to feel "that sensual involvement with the opposite sex burned bright and hot with unquenchable passion and at the same time that any such involvement was utterly repulsive," she may well have approached her prospective partners "as if she were picking up a live coal in one hand and a dead rat in the other" (*White over Black*).

One need not take Jordan's analogy beyond the figurative dimensions it is meant to encompass to see the distortions of passion miscegenation could produce in whites as well as blacks—distortions that entirely depended upon one another and, as . . . in the case of *Light in August*, eventually produced a hysterical climate of racial fantasy that would make the repression and denial of miscegenation more necessary than ever. The distinctions that have to be made between Joanna Burden and Rosa Coldfield are no doubt important, but they depend less on psychology than temporality; that is, the movement back from the tragedy of Jim Crow to the tragedy of slavery that Faulkner's extending of the theme of miscegenation necessitated is one that required him to dramatize the initial crisis of blood and identity out of which its later manifestations had grown. The "*unravished nuptial*" in which Rosa lives along with Judith (and, it seems, Clytie), the "*one constant and perpetual instant when the arras-veil before what-is-to-be*" awaits "*the lightest naked thrust,*" the "*cocoon-casket marriage-bed of youth and grief*" she lies down in once and forever in 1860, the long relived and remembered "*might-have-been which is more than truth*"—these singular moments of a marriage that was never to be acquire their energizing power from the fact that, leaving aside altogether the question of Rosa's knowledge of Bon's blood, we have to read them as revealing a desire for Bon the novel itself must express, even if it can do so only indirectly or unconsciously. Exactly because these moments are offered up in the realm of remembered fantasy, Rosa's Gothic eroticism contains a virulent nostalgia and willful innocence that betray the dark underside of slaveholding marriage: that white women often lived in the face of a monstrous affront and—more alarming indeed— may well have had passions of their own. The children of miscegenation not only threatened to blur the distinctions that made slavery possible, but the unions that produced them threatened to distort sexual relations and marriage itself, for black and white alike, into peculiar and tragic forms.

In the year before the war, Rosa says, "*Ellen talked to me of trousseau (and it my trousseau), of all the dreamy panoply of surrender which was my surrender*"; when the news of Lincoln's election and the fall of Sumter comes, Rosa is sewing "for her own vicarious bridal" the garments that she "would never wear and never remove for a man whom she was not even to see," still sewing when Mississippi secedes and the regiment commanded by Sutpen and Sartoris appears in town beneath regimental colors "sewed together out of silk dresses." The superimposing of these actions is a symbolic expression of their relentless entanglement in *Absalom, Absalom!* Still sewing those marital garments in memory, and still unable to put them on or take them off forty-five years later—later still when Faulkner writes the book we read—Rosa lives in a world of tortured innocence that is only conceivable because it is, in this case more than ever, the product of a superannuated guilt. That guilt is not necessarily Rosa's, but it is Faulkner's (as author) and it is the South's. The fevered moment of union she lives in still, distended by the ruinous divisions that bring it into being, is haunting in extremity: it is a moment in which she cannot, will not, will never "surrender." For reasons absolutely dependent upon the tragic realities of miscegenation, Rosa's marriage to Bon that never was is a crucial part of the failure of Sutpen's design—crucial because it illuminates the mockery of Sutpen's actual marriages to Eulalia Bon and Ellen Coldfield and the one he proposes to Rosa.

No tragedy is greater than Bon's or Clytie's or that of their mothers, but Rosa's brings them into perspective, not only by uniting them but also by diffusing their shadows through and into the intimate heart of the slave-holding South and its unsurrendering memories. The greater passions Rosa and Faulkner express in her extraordinary disembodied meditation on the world of lost love are nearly unaccountable unless we take seriously the unsettling dimensions of sexual union to which they refer, dimensions in which sexuality became split between love and lust, and in which familial and affectionate relations of every kind could be torn from their natural paths of development and turned into grotesque reflections of the institution they supported. As Frederick Douglass reported in 1845, the slaveholder, in sustaining "to his slaves the double relation of master and father," at once indulged his wicked desires, increased his property, inspired the contempt and cruelty of his wife, and left himself subject to acts of extreme emotional estrangement. Cruel as it may seem "for a man to sell his own children to human flesh-mongers," wrote Douglass, he must otherwise "not only whip them himself, but must stand by and see one white son tie up his brother, of but a few shades darker complexion than himself, and ply the gory lash to his naked back (*Narrative of the Life of Frederick Douglass*). One can measure the achievement of *Absalom, Absalom!* no more clearly than by noting with what inspired passion, and without capitulating either to sentimentality or to bitterness, it works against the violent limitations such a situation placed on human love.

Faulkner's novel can express that love only by remarkable indirection—most significantly, . . . in the re-creations of Quentin and Shreve, but most passionately (and therefore most indirectly) in the pressures that culminate in Rosa's unravished nuptial, the mock marriage that in its reciprocal affirmation and denial of love most ably characterizes the central emotional tragedies of slavery. As Rosa sews her trousseau, the conflict that will suspend all actions and decisions for four years begins. The murder and the design it will at once preserve and destroy are held in suspense while the South seeks, in magnificent fashion, to deny its union with the nation and the North seeks, in fashions devised by Lincoln, to restore union without abolishing slavery. Neither plan will work; the price for both the South and the North is the story Faulkner will still tell more than half a century later when, dividing his novel in half, he shifts its burden from Rosa Coldfield, widow, to Quentin Compson, suicide, one of the characters he "had to get out of the attic to tell the story of Sutpen."

Incredulous Narration:
Absalom, Absalom!

Peter Brooks

To a reader concerned with the design and project of narrative, William Faulkner's *Absalom, Absalom!* is full of interest. More than Faulkner's other novels, *Absalom, Absalom!* seems to pose with acute force problems in the epistemology of narrative and the cognitive uses of plotting in a context of radical doubt about the validity of plot. Perhaps even more than such cerebral probes into these issues as Joyce's *Ulysses*, Gide's *Les Faux-Monnayeurs*, Italo Svevo's *La Coscienza di Zeno*, or Michel Butor's *La Modification*, *Absalom, Absalom!* offers an exemplary challenge to the critic since it both sums up the nineteenth-century tradition of the novel—particularly its concern with genealogy, authority, and patterns of transmission—while subverting it, working this subversion in a manner that reaffirms a traditional set of problems for the novel while disallowing its traditional solutions. Here is a novel that in its appendix provides us with a chronology (as in Freud's final footnote to the Wolf Man), a genealogy (as in such familial chronicles as Zola's *Les Rougon-Macquart* and Galsworthy's *The Forsyte Saga*), and a map (furnished implicitly if not literally throughout Balzac, Tolstoy, Hardy, and other novelists who stake out and order terrain). These are traditional schemata for the ordering of time and experience from which *Absalom, Absalom!* markedly departs, yet by which it is also haunted, as by the force of an absence. *Absalom, Absalom!* may indeed be very much the story of the haunting force of absences, including formal absences, in the wake of whose passage the novel constructs itself.

From *Reading for the Plot: Design and Intention in Narrative.* © 1984 by Peter Brooks. Knopf, 1984.

As a first approach to the place of plot in *Absalom, Absalom!*, we can refer again to the concept of narrative as a coded activity, implicit in all narratology and urged most persuasively by Roland Barthes in *S/Z*. That is, a given narrative weaves its individual pattern from preexistent codes, which derive, most immediately at least, from the "already written." The reading of a narrative then tends to decipher, to organize, to rationalize, to *name* in terms of codes derived from the "already read." . . . Two of Barthes's five codes seem particularly pertinent to the study of plot: the proairetic, or "code of actions," and the hermeneutic, or code of enigmas and answers, ultimately the code or voice of "Truth." The proairetic . . . concerns the logic of actions, how the completion of an action can be logically derived from its initiation, and the whole of an action seen as a complete and namable unit, which then enters into combination with other actions, to form sequences. Like its label, this code is essentially Aristotelian, concerned with the wholeness of actions and the logic of their interrelationship. The hermeneutic code rather concerns the questions and answers that structure a story, their suspense, partial unveiling, temporary blockage, eventual resolution, with the resultant creation of a "retarding structure" or "dilatory space" which we work through toward what is felt, in classical narrative, to be meaning revealed. Plot . . . might best be conceived as a combination of the proairetic and the hermeneutic, or better, an over-coding of the proairetic by the hermeneutic. The actions and sequences of action of the narrative are structured into larger wholes by the play of enigma and solution: the hermeneutic acts as a large, shaping force, allowing us to sort out, to group, to see the significance of actions, to rename their sequences in terms of their significance for the narrative as a whole. We read in the suspense created by the hermeneutic code, structuring actions according to its indications, restructuring as we move through partial revelations and misleading clues, moving toward the fullness of meaning provided by the "saturation" of the matrix of the sentence now fully predicated.

A major source of our difficulty in reading *Absalom, Absalom!* may derive from its peculiar use of these two codes, the way they refuse to mesh or synchronize in the traditional mode. As readers, we encounter in the novel certain sequences of action and event that seem to lack any recognizable framework of question and answer, and hence any clear intention of meaning. Worse still, we encounter sequences where the orderly progression of the "proairetisms," the movement of chains of events to their conclusion, is interrupted and interfered with by the formulation of enigmas concerning the actions themselves. It is as if the characters in the novel often turned to the interrogation of a proairetic sequence for its revelatory meaning before we, as readers, have been allowed to see how the sequence runs. The very logic of action is violated by the inquiry into its hermeneutic force, an inquiry that can only derive its sense from an end to the sequence which we have not been privileged to see. Thus it is that we so often find ourselves suddenly faced with hermeneutic shifts of gears, forced to reconsider the very integrity of narrative event in terms of its hermeneutic possibilities and determinations; so that we often find ourselves in the position of Quentin Compson's Canadian roommate at Harvard, Shreve McCannon (relatively, of course, the outsider in the narrative), wanting to shout, as he does, "Wait! For God's sake wait." One quite straightforward instance of the situation I have in mind occurs in the narrative of the killing of Thomas Sutpen by Wash Jones after the birth of the child fathered by Sutpen on Wash's daughter, Milly Jones, where we have this exchange between Shreve and Quentin:

> "Wait," Shreve said. "You mean that he got the son he wanted, after all that trouble, and then turned right around and—"
>
> "Yes. Sitting in Grandfather's office that afternoon, with his head kind of flung back a little, explaining to Grandfather like he might have been explaining arithmetic to Henry back in the fourth grade: 'You see, all I wanted was just a son. Which seems to me, when I look about at my contemporary scene, no exorbitant gift from nature or circumstance to demand—' "
>
> "*Will you wait?*" Shreve said. "—that with the son he went to all that trouble to get lying right there behind him in the cabin, he would have to taunt the grandfather into killing first him and then the child too?"
>
> "—What?" Quentin said. "It wasn't a son. It was a girl."
>
> "Oh," Shreve said. "—Come on. Let's get out of this damn icebox and go to bed."

We find here a suspension of the revelation that is necessary to make the actions previously recounted (Sutpen's refusal to marry or even to provide for Milly since she has produced a daughter, not a son) into some version of Barthes's fully predicated narrative sentence. This suspension heightens—at the expense of "meaning"—the dramatic rendering of what is the final destruction of Sutpen's life-plot, his "design," itself a major shaping force in the overall hermeneutic code of the narrative.

The reader just as often finds himself witness to a proairetic sequence that appears perfectly logical but lacks the coherence of meaning, as if he had not been given the hermeneutic clues requisite to grasping the intention of event and the motive of its narration. The reader in these cases stands in much the same position as Quentin at the outset of the novel, listening to Rosa Coldfield's narration. I cite a fragment of her narrative from the early pages:

> "I saw what had happened to Ellen, my sister. I saw her almost a recluse, watching those two doomed children growing up whom she was helpless to save. I saw the price which she had paid for that house and that pride; I saw the notes of hand on pride and contentment and peace and all to which she had put her signature when she walked into the church that night, begin to fall due in succession. I saw Judith's marriage forbidden without rhyme or reason or shadow of excuse; I saw Ellen die with only me, a child, to turn to and ask to protect her remaining child; I saw Henry repudiate his home and birthright and then return and practically fling the bloody corpse of his sister's sweetheart at the hem of her wedding gown; I saw that man return— the evil's source and head which had outlasted all its victims— who had created two children not only to destroy one another and his own line, but my line as well, yet I agreed to marry him."

This passage in fact gives virtually the whole of the story to be told, from Rosa's point of view, and gives it with the insistent veracity of the eyewitness account: "I saw . . . I saw." What is missing from her account? In some important sense, everything, for it is a largely nonhermeneutic narrative, offering no apparent structure of meaning for this sequence of events, indeed no clue as to how and even why one should look for meaning in it. There is narrative aplenty here, as throughout the novel, but inadequate *grounds* for narrative.

One might generalize from this quotation, to suggest that it characterizes not only a problem *in* the narrative, but the very problem *of* narrative in *Absalom, Absalom!*, where ultimately narrative itself is the problem. Mr. Compson typically generalizes the problem for us, in one of his noble but slightly futile epic evocations:

> "It's just incredible. It just does not explain. Or perhaps that's it: they don't explain and we are not supposed to know. We have a few old mouth-to-mouth tales; we exhume from old trunks and boxes and drawers letters without salutation or sig-

nature, in which men and women who once lived and breathed are now merely initials or nicknames out of some now incomprehensible affection which sound to us like Sanskrit or Chocktaw; we see dimly people, the people in whose living blood and seed we ourselves lay dormant and waiting, in this shadowy attenuation of time possessing now heroic proportions, performing their acts of simple passion and simple violence, impervious to time and inexplicable—Yes, Judith, Bon, Henry, Sutpen: all of them. They are there, yet something is missing; they are like a chemical formula exhumed along with the letters from that forgotten chest, carefully, the paper old and faded and falling to pieces, the writing faded, almost indecipherable, yet meaningful, familiar in shape and sense, the name and presence of volatile and sentient forces; you bring them together in the proportions called for, but nothing happens; you re-read, tedious and intent, poring, making sure that you have forgotten nothing, made no miscalculation; you bring them together again and again nothing happens: just the words, the symbols, the shapes themselves, shadowy inscrutable and serene, against that turgid background of a horrible and bloody mischancing of human affairs."

This passage alludes to all the enigmatic issues of the narrative: Why did Henry Sutpen kill Charles Bon? What did this killing have to do with Thomas Sutpen, and with the eventual ruin of the house of Sutpen? What does this tale of the ancestors have to do with the present generations? And, especially, how can narrative know what happened and make sense of the motives of events? And if it cannot, what happens to lines of descent, to the transmission of knowledge and wisdom, and to history itself? Is history finally simply a "bloody mischancing of human affairs"? If for Barthes the resolution of all enigmas coincides with the full and final predication of the narrative sentence, Mr. Compson here appears to question the possibility of ever finding a predicate: the subjects—the proper names—are there, but they refuse to accede to meaning.

The quotations from Rosa Coldfield and Mr. Compson both tend to suggest that on the one hand there is a story to be told—perhaps even history itself to be told—and on the other hand there is telling and writing—people writing and reading letters and documents, and especially, talking—but that somehow what should lie in-between, the story-as-told, the narrative as coherently plotted, the hermeneutic sentence, is lacking. Referring . . . to Gérard Genette's categories, *histoire, récit,* and *narration*—"story," "plot," and "narrating"—it is evident that in *Absalom, Absalom!* we have on the one hand plenty of narrating, and on the other at least the postulation of a story that may equal history itself. What appears to be missing is the level of plot, the result of Mr. Compson's chemical operation, that comprehensible order of event that was the very substance and raison d'être of the classical narrative.

Another way of stating the problem might be to say that in this novel which preeminently concerns fathers, sons, generation, and lines of descent, there seems to be no clear authority, not even of a provisional sort, for the telling of the story, and as a result no suggestion of how to achieve mastery of its interpretation. The nineteenth-century novel . . . repeatedly concerns issues of authority and transmission, and regularly plays them out in relations of fathers to sons. From Rousseau to Freud, the discourse of the self and its origins—so much a matter of patronymics—ultimately concerns the authority of identity, that knowledge of self which, through all its complex workings-out, aims at the demonstrative statement, "this is what I am." *Absalom, Absalom!* problematizes further this classic issue in that not only does the identity of all the important characters seem to be in question, but the very discourse about identity seems to lack authority. As we have argued in discussion of the narrative situation, stories are told in the name of something or someone; they are told *for* something. The incessant narrating of *Absalom, Absalom!*, however, seems to bring us perilously close to narrative without motive: a collection of "letters without salutation or signature," unable to name their sender or receiver, and unable to define the subject of their narrative discourse. If we ever are to be able to define the status of plot in this novel, we will first have to discover the motives of storytelling. Narrative meaning very much depends on the *uses* of narrative.

These formulations may begin to take on more precise and more useful meaning if I now return to the beginning of the novel, and attempt for the moment to be more explicative. We have at the outset a teller and a listener, or narrator and narratee. Rosa is doing the telling, "in that grim haggard amazed voice until at last listening would renege and hearing-sense self-confound and the long-dead object of her impotent yet indomitable frustration would appear, as though by outraged recapitulation evoked." This description could stand as emblem for all of Rosa's narrating, and indeed for much of the storytelling in the novel: an evocation through outraged recapitulation, where there is evidently a need not only to remember but also—in Freud's terms—to repeat and to "work through" an as yet unmastered past, from motives that are highly charged emotionally but not specified or yet specifiable. Nor does the listener, Quentin, know why he has been chosen as Rosa's narratee, so that we have from the outset an interrogation of the motive and intention of telling. *"It's because she wants it told,* he thought, *so that people whom she will never see and whose names she will never hear and who will never have heard her name nor seen her face will read it and know at last why God let us lose the War."* Quentin's explanation here leaps over what we might have expected to be a formulation of the storyteller's intention in terms of the coherent design given to her story by its shaping plot, leaps to the level of history, to the *fabula* as something truly fabulous: the epic of the Civil War, the tragedy of southern history. The war and the history of the South may in some ultimate sense be both the final principle of explanation for everyone in the novel, and the final problem needing explanation. But to make a direct leap to that level is to elide the intervening level of plot, of coherently motivated and shaped narrative: between story as history on the one hand, and the recapitulative narrating on the other, plot seems to have been lost, to have failed in its role as the cohesive bond of the narrative construction.

It is worth noting that this initial situation of telling in *Absalom, Absalom!*, which places face to face the one surviving eyewitness to the past (or so we, and Quentin, believe at this point) and the representative of the future, he who is supposed to escape the South, is hermeneutically most significant at the point—the very end of chapter 1—where we are given the fragment of a narrative of what Rosa did *not* see: "But I was not there. I was not there to see the two Sutpen faces this time—once on Judith and once on the negro girl beside her—looking down through the square entrance to the loft." This is far more consequential for a construction of the plot than Rosa's recapitulation of her moral outrage at Sutpen's wrestling bouts with his slaves, which Judith and Clytie are watching from the loft: it is not the seen but the seers, unseen by the eyewitness, which constitute our hermeneutic clue here. For in the doubling of Judith in Clytie, in the Negro version of Sutpen, lies the very trace of difference which is the ironic determinant of Sutpen's plot.

But this is a clue that can only be interpreted later. By the close of the first chapter, I have suggested, there is a split and a polarization: narrating on the one hand, an epic historical story on the other; and no narrative plot or design to join them. In this structure of the absent middle, the failed mediation, the problem of the rest of the novel is formulated: How can we construct the plot? Who can say it? To whom? On what authority? The narrative of *Absalom, Absalom!* not only raises these issues, it actively pursues them. The novel becomes a kind of detective story where the object of investigation—the mystery—is the narrative design, or plot, itself.

We might note briefly the forms in which this problem develops over the succeeding chapters. In chapters 2, 3, and 4, Mr. Compson is telling. (One hesitates to label him, or any other of the tellers, a "narrator" in the traditional sense, since narration here as elsewhere in Faulkner seems to call upon both the individual's voice and that transindividual voice that speaks through all of Faulkner's characters. Certainly the narrative is "focalized" by an individual—to use Genette's terminology again—but the question of voice is more difficult to resolve.) Mr. Compson is eminently the figure of transmission, standing between his father, General Compson, the nearest thing to a friend that Sutpen had in Jefferson, and his son Quentin. Mr. Compson fills in some of the background of Sutpen's story, his arrival in Jefferson, his marriage to Ellen Coldfield, the birth of the two children, Judith and Henry, the appearance of Charles Bon. Chapter 3 ends with the evocation of Wash Jones appearing before Rosa's house to tell of Henry's shooting of Bon; then, curiously, chapter 4 ends with the same moment, but with Wash Jones's message fully articulated this time: "Henry has done shot that durn French feller. Kilt him dead as a beef." The two chapter endings force us to ask what has happened in the intervening pages to advance our understanding of this killing, which from Rosa's initial presentation of the elements of the story has stood as a shocking challenge to understanding.

What we have had, essentially, is the elaboration of Mr. Compson's plot, involving Henry and Bon and Judith. It turns on Bon's earlier morganatic marriage to the octoroon woman in New Orleans, making of him an "intending bigamist" in the betrothal to Judith. Mr. Compson is a rich scenarist, imaging the meeting of Henry and Bon at the University of Mississippi, Henry's "seduction" by Bon, the scenes at Sutpen's Hundred during vacations, Henry's trip to New Orleans, and so on. It is a narrative in which we are ever passing from the postulation of how it must have been to the conviction that it really was that way: for instance, Mr. Compson imagines the introduction of Henry to Bon in a series of clauses headed "perhaps," ending: "or perhaps (I like to think this) presented formally to the man reclining in a flowered, almost feminized gown, in a sunny window in his chambers," and then a page later has turned the hypothesis into solid narrative event: "And the very fact that, lounging before them in the outlandish and almost feminine garments of his sybaritic privacy." And yet, for all his evident will to construct a hermeneutically powerful plot, Mr. Compson encounters moments of radical doubt, most notably in the passage beginning, "It just does not explain," which I quoted earlier. We have a complex, intricate, seemingly highly motivated plot that ultimately appears to get the story of Bon and Henry all wrong. Like Rosa's narrative, however, Mr. Compson's does include some important hermeneutic clues hidden in its mistaken design: the issue of incest, for instance, is suggested in the relation of Henry and Judith—in the vicarious incest Henry would enjoy in Bon's marriage to Judith, whom Mr. Compson does not suspect to be related by blood—and the issue of miscegenation is posed by the very existence of the octoroon woman. These are latent figures of narrative design which will later provide some of the hermeneutic "chemistry" that Mr. Compson's plotting is unable to activate.

With chapter 5, we return to Rosa's telling, and a nearer approach to the moment of murder. "I heard an echo, but not the shot," she says, in a phrase emblematic of her whole relation to narrative event, which is one of secondariness and bafflement. Her narrating takes us precisely to what she did not see and cannot tell: the confrontation of Henry and Judith over Bon's corpse. Imagining the dialogue of brother and sister falls to her listener, Quentin; and we can infer that this need to tell will provide his entry into the narrative structure of the novel more directly than will Rosa's revelation that there is someone other than Clytie currently living at Sutpen's Hundred:

> the two of them, brother and sister . . . speaking to one another
> in short brief staccato sentences like slaps. . . .
> *Now you cant marry him.*
> *Why cant I marry him?*
> *Because he's dead.*
> *Dead?*
> *Yes. I killed him.*
> He (Quentin) couldn't pass that. He was not even listening
> to her; he said "Ma'am? What's that? What did you say?"
> "There's something in that house."
> "In that house? It's Clytie. Dont she—"
> "No. Something living in it. Hidden in it. It has been out
> there for four years, living hidden in that house."

What is living in the house is, of course, Henry Sutpen, and Quentin's meeting with him, a few hours following this exchange with Rosa, will possibly constitute the most important event of the story that needs telling in *Absalom, Absalom!* and the key motive of its plot, as well as the original impetus to Quentin's narrating. But representation of this event is deferred until the very last pages of the novel. Here, at the close of Rosa's narrative, the narratee—Quentin—appears to fix on one moment of the narrator's account (why is a question we may defer for now) which he cannot "pass."

Since, he seems to imply, the narrator has not done justice to this moment, it is up to the narratee to pursue its true narrative implications and consequences. If we may later want to say that Quentin enters the Sutpen *story* through the meeting with Henry at Sutpen's Hundred, he enters the *narrative* on the plane of *narrating,* as the better artist of the narrative plot. Yet, by what right and in what interest does Quentin claim the role of narrator? And if the listener/narratee has moved into the position of narrator, who has come to occupy the position he has vacated?

From chapter 6 through to the end of the novel, the narrating will essentially be Quentin's. His ostensible narratee will be Shreve, yet Shreve will come to participate in the narrating to such an extent that he too must eventually be considered a narrator. The agency of narration will hence be fully dialogic, which both solves and evades the question of the vacancy created by Quentin's movement into the place of the narrator. We need at this point to ask what kind of a narrative principle and authority is provided, can be provided, by these two young men who have usurped narrating, de-authorized the eyewitness account (Rosa's) and the account at one remove (Mr. Compson's) in favor of something at greater distance (both temporally and spatially) but which claims greater hermeneutic force. We need to ask three straightforward, quite naive questions: What do they recount? How do they know it? What is their motive, their investment in what they recount?

Let me start with the second question, that of the epistemology of their narrative. As source for their narrative, there is first of all something in the nature of "documentary evidence." Chapters 6 through 9 in fact are framed by Mr. Compson's letter recounting Rosa's death and burial, and earlier Mr. Compson had shown Quentin the letter Judith had given Quentin's grandmother, the letter written to Judith by Charles Bon in captured Yankee stovepolish in 1865. Then there are the tombstones, as so often in the nineteenth-century novel—in *Great Expectations,* for instance, and in Wilkie Collins's *The Woman in White*—authoritative texts that nonetheless require decipherment. Quentin and his father, out shooting quail at Sutpen's Hundred, come upon five tombstones. These are: (1) Ellen's (ordered from Italy, brought home by Sutpen in 1864); (2) Sutpen's own (of the same provenance); (3) Charles Bon's (bought by Judith when she sold the store); (4) Charles Etienne Saint-Valery Bon's (paid for partly by Judith, partly by General Compson, and erected by the latter); (5) Judith's (provided by Rosa). The aberrant and enigmatic text here—hence the clue—is the fourth tombstone, that of Charles Etienne Saint-Valery Bon (Charles Bon's child by the octoroon woman), who looks white but chooses blackness: who takes a black wife (their child will be the idiot Jim Bond), and in fact has black ancestry in both his mother *and* his father, though we do not yet know this. This Bon, who is hauled into court after a fight and admonished by the justice, Jim Hamblett, for "going with blacks," in fact presents a problem in categorization: Hamblett, following the vocative "you, a white man," turns back on his words to find the sign he has used subverted in its referent: "he looking at the prisoner now but saying 'white' again even while his voice died away as if the order to stop the voice had been shocked into short circuit, '*What are you? Who and where did you come from?*' " In this slippage of signified from under its signifier, we encounter a transgression of categories and accepted patternings which provides an essential trace of hermeneutic design.

More important than the documentary evidence is oral transmission. Quentin's main source of knowledge comes from what Sutpen told his grandfather, General Compson, during the hunt for the French architect, and then on another occasion thirty years later when he came to General Compson's office, a narrative which General Compson passed on to Mr. Compson who passed it on to Quentin. But his narrative lacks meaning until it is retroactively completed by what Quentin himself learns from his visit to Sutpen's Hundred with Rosa in 1909:

> "Your father," Shreve said. "He seems to have got an awful lot of delayed information awful quick, after having waited forty-five years. If he knew all this, what was his reason for telling you that the trouble between Henry and Bon was the octoroon woman?"
>
> "He didn't know it then. Grandfather didn't tell him all of it either, like Sutpen never told Grandfather quite all of it."
>
> "Then who did tell him?"
>
> "I did." Quentin did not move, did not look up while Shreve watched him. "The day after we—after that night when we—"
>
> "Oh," Shreve said. "After you and the old aunt. I see."

This dialogue marks the supersession of Mr. Compson's, General Compson's, even Sutpen's own narratives in favor of Quentin's, since Quentin has been able to supply essential "delayed information" previously missing, thus creating a narrative that has retroactive explanatory force. The nature of this information is further specified a few pages later:

> "Your old man," Shreve said. "When your grandfather was telling this to him, he didn't know any more what your grand-

father was talking about than your grandfather knew what the
demon was talking about when the demon told it to him, did
he? And when your old man told it to you, you wouldn't have
known what anybody was talking about if you hadn't been out
there and seen Clytie. Is that right?"

"Yes," Quentin said.

This information, then, does not come from anything Quentin has read or
been told, but simply from seeing Clytie. Here, a decisive clue finally is
witnessed and interpreted by an adequate narrator. Clytie, who in Rosa's
words *"in the very pigmentation of her flesh represented that debacle which had
brought Judith and me to what we were,"* is a Negro Sutpen. Clytie's identity
opens the possibility of other part-Negro Sutpen children and alerts the
narrators (and readers) to the significant strain of miscegenation; it also sets
a model of narrative repetition which will allow Quentin and Shreve to see
how Henry and Bon will be acting out Sutpen's script, but in the mode of
irony. It is Quentin—the narratee become narrator—who will eventually
be able to postulate the essential discovery: that Charles Bon was also
Sutpen's child, and that he, too, was part Negro. The source of that postulation, we should emphasize, is the discovery of a certain formal pattern
of the crossing of categories: Clytie's Sutpen face with its Negro pigmentation, the very design of debacle. The "truth" of narrative may have come
to depend, more than on any fact, on powerful formal patternings, designs,
eventually, of the narrative itself; a question to which we shall return.

I have by no means said all that needs to be said about the epistemological issues of Quentin's and Shreve's narrative, but I want for a moment
to return to the first of the three questions I identified, the question of what
they recount. The story they tell is in the first instance, and essentially, that
of Sutpen, which has come to appear the necessary myth of origins of all
the problems under consideration, and which in itself very much concerns
origins. It has become apparent that nothing can be solved or explained
without getting Sutpen's story straight. We could say that it has become
apparent that horizontal relationships, those of siblingship and courtship—
Judith, Bon, Henry—which were at the center of Mr. Compson's narrative
have come to show their hermeneutic inadequacy and their insolubility in
isolation. As Quentin reflects, in one of several meditations on the inescapable issue of paternity: *"Yes, we are both Father. Or maybe Father and I
are both Shreve, maybe it took Father and me both to make Shreve or Shreve and
me both to make Father or maybe Thomas Sutpen to make all of us."* Consideration must now be directed to a vertical problem, an issue in genealogy
and the transmission of paternal authority through historical time.

Sutpen's story, filled in mainly in chapter 7, has its thematic summary in the statement, "Sutpen's trouble was innocence." It is the story of a hillbilly boy from the mountains who comes down to the tidewater with his family and is sent by his father to a plantation house with a message, only to be turned away from the front door and told to come round to the back. In this moment of barred passage, Sutpen discovers the existence of difference: difference as an abstract and formal property which takes precedence over all else—since, for instance, it is more important than the content of the message he was supposed to deliver. Good and evil, morality, social position, worth are not substantial, but belong rather to the order of the signifier. The scenario reads like a version of Rousseau's *Discourse on the Origins of Inequality:* the creation of possession and differentiation where previously there had been none. The difference is symbolized by that between black and white, though this is but the most immediate and visible realization of a larger problem, one indeed so basic that even the boy Sutpen can begin to understand its primordial role in the organization and assignment of meaning. Sutpen's compensatory plot, what he repeatedly calls his "design," will be conceived to assure his place on the proper side of the bar of difference. He goes off to Haiti to make his fortune on a sugar plantation, and there takes a wife who he believes to be part French and part Spanish, but who—after she has borne his son—is revealed to be part Negro, a fact that, as he puts it, makes an "ironic delusion" of his entire design, which depends upon genealogical clarity and purity, on the ability to chart a clear authoritative relationship between origin and endpoint. So Sutpen repudiates his wife and starts over again at Sutpen's Hundred, in a new originating creation: "creating the Sutpen's Hundred, the *Be Sutpen's Hundred* like the olden-time *Be Light.*" But then, his son by the first wife, Charles Bon, appears from the past to threaten "a mockery and a betrayal" of his design: asking through the vessel of Judith that the new pure Sutpen line be intermixed with the dark blood of the past. So it is that Sutpen must turn Charles Bon, his first-born son, from the front door of his own plantation house. In the wake of all disasters, Sutpen goes on trying: after the war, and the disappearance of Henry, he proposes to Rosa that they breed together, then marry if she produces a son. After she has fled back to Jefferson in outrage, he makes a last attempt with Milly Jones—poor white, but white—which results in a daughter, and Sutpen's death at the hand of Wash Jones.

I have dwelt on Sutpen's "design" because it is a key not only to the overriding thematic issues of the novel but, more important, to the symbolic field in which it inscribes its reflection on narrative meaning. Sutpen himself is a master-plotter, endowed with an abstract, formalist sense of what the future shape of his life must be. Yet his repeated attempts to found a genealogy do not work, no doubt because one cannot postulate the authority and outcome of a genealogy from its origin. The authority of genealogy is known only in its outcome, in its *issue*, using that word in all its possible senses. Sutpen attempts to write the history of the House of Sutpen prospectively, whereas history is evidently always retrospective. I have indeed argued that all narrative must, as a system of meaning, conceive itself as essentially retrospective. Only the sons can tell the story of the fathers. Narrative, like genealogy, is a matter of patronymics. And here we may find both a source of Quentin's relative success as narrator of the past and a source of his anguish at being condemned to narrate the past, the world of ghosts which has fallen to his inheritance and which one can attempt to placate only through acts of genealogical narration.

When Quentin and Shreve have given shape to Sutpen's story, they turn to Sutpen's immediate issue, to the sons, Bon and Henry. Bon, too, we learn, has a design. Its parodic form—a parody of all the plots in the novel—is represented by the figure of Bon's mother's lawyer, scheming to blackmail Sutpen through the threat of incest, maintaining his secret notations:

> *Today Sutpen finished robbing a drunken Indian of a hundred miles of virgin land, val. $25,000. At 2:31 today came up out of swamp with final plank for house, val. in conj. with land 40,000. 7:52 p.m. today married. Bigamy threat val. minus nil. unless quick buyer. Not probable. Doubtless conjoined with wife same day. Say 1 year* and then with maybe the date and the hour too: *Son. Intrinsic val. possible though not probable forced sale of house & land plus val. crop minus child's one quarter. Emotional val. plus 100% times nil. plus val. crop. Say 10 years, one or more children. Intrinsic val. forced sale house & improved land plus liquid assets minus children's share. Emotional val. 100% times increase yearly for each child plus intrinsic val. plus liquid assets plus working acquired credit* and maybe here with the date too: *Daughter* and you could maybe even have seen the question mark after it and the other words even: *daughter? daughter? daughter?* trailing off.

The lawyer's calculations here devastatingly lay bare the plot of the nineteenth-century social and familial novel, with its equations of consanguinity, property, ambition, and eros, that is ever the backdrop for the plottings of *Absalom, Absalom!* Yet Bon appears as the hero of romance, with a simpler and more absolute design. He simply wants a sign—any sign—of recognition from his father. "*He would just have to write 'I am your father. Burn this' and I would do it.*" Bon's insistence on marriage to Judith becomes the choice of scandal in order to force the admission of paternity. What appears to be erotic desire reveals itself to be founded on the absolute demand for recognition by the father.

The working-out of Bon's design leads to the key scene, in 1865, as the Confederate army falls back toward Richmond and final defeat, when Colonel Sutpen summons Henry to his tent and speaks the essential words: "*Henry, . . . my son*"—the words Bon will never hear—and delivers the final answer to the enigma, completes the hermeneutic sentence that should allow us to explain the mischancings of the affairs of the House of Sutpen: "*He must not marry her, Henry. His mother's father told me that her mother had been a Spanish woman. I believed him; it was not until after he was born that I found out that his mother was part negro.*" And Bon draws the conclusion: "*So it's the miscegenation, not the incest, which you cant bear.*" Thus it is that at this belated point in the novel, knowledge catches up with event, and Henry, along with the reader, learns what those narrators who originally were narratees have learned.

But wait. On what basis and by what authority do Quentin and Shreve narrate this scene, the scene that articulates the revelations necessary to constructing a coherent plot? Whereas for many earlier parts of their narrative we glimpsed sources and documents, here there are none. Indeed, the narrators have clearly passed beyond any possible evidence for their narrative. As Shreve has stated some pages earlier, "Let me play a while now." And before that, "All right. Dont bother to say he stopped talking now; just go on." These and a number of other indications signal clearly that we have passed beyond any narrative reporting, to narrative invention; that narrating, having failed to construct from the evidence a plot that would make sense of the story, turn to inventing it. Even what we normally call "reported speech"—direct quotation—is the product of an act of ventriloquism, in a duet for four voices in which Quentin and Shreve become compounded with Henry and Bon, "compounded each of both yet either neither." To the question, Who is speaking here? the text replies, Everyone and no one:

> It might have been either of them and was in a sense both: both
> thinking as one, the voice which happened to be speaking the
> thought only the thinking become audible, vocal; the two of
> them creating between them, out of the rag-tag and bob-ends
> of old tales and talking, people who perhaps had never existed

at all anywhere, who, shadows, were shadows not of flesh and blood which had lived and died but shadows in turn of what were (to one of them at least, to Shreve) shades too, quiet as the visible murmur of their vaporizing breath.

What can this mean, if not that the narratees/listeners/readers have taken over complete responsibility for the narrative, and that the "voice of the reader" has evicted all other voices from the text, eliminated all the syntactic subordinations of reportage ("He said that she said that . . .") in favor of a direct re-creation, and has set itself up, by a supreme act of usurpation, as the sole authority of narrative? Commenting on a particularly ambiguous case of voicing in Balzac's *Sarrasine,* Barthes reaches the conclusion that ultimately the voice that speaks in the text is that of the reader, in that it is in the reader's interest, in his name, that the story must be told. Here, as narrators, narratees, and characters become compounded and interchangeable—and the narrated and the narrating occupy shifting positions—we have very nearly a literal realization of Barthes's point: the distance between telling and listening, between writing and reading, has collapsed; the reader has been freed to speak in the text, toward the creation of the text.

The passage quoted shows us how narration can become fully dialogic, centerless, a transaction across what may be a referential void—filled perhaps only with phantasies from the past—yet a transaction that creates, calls into being, a necessary hermeneutic fiction. The narrative transaction thus appears fully consonant with the psychoanalytic transference, a *Zwischenreich* in which narration works through and works out a narrative solution. Furthermore, here the transferential dialogue is carried out by those who were originally narratees and readers, as if the analysts had also become analysands, assuming the burden of all stories, as also the power to reorder them correctly. To the literary analyst, this may imply that the reader, like Quentin and Shreve, will always take over the text, both reading and (re)-writing it to his own design, finding in it "what will suffice" to his own hermeneutic need and desire. As Bon's desire once postulated develops by the dynamics of its own internal tension toward the scene in Sutpen's tent in 1865, so the reader's desire inhabits the text and strives toward the fulfillment of interpretation. A further, more radical implication might be that the implied occurrences or events of the story (in the sense of *fabula*) are merely a by-product of the needs of plot, indeed of plotting, of the rhetoric of the *sjužet:* that one need no longer worry about the "double logic" of narrative since event is merely a necessary illusion that enables the interpretive narrative discourse to go further, as in the mind of some Borgesian demiurge. This in turn might imply that the ultimate subject of any narrative is its narrating, that narrative inevitably reveals itself to be a Moebius strip where we unwittingly end up on the plane from which we began. Origin and endpoint—and, perforce, genealogy and history—are merely as-if postulations ultimately subject to the arbitrary whims of the agency of narration, and of its model in readership. Narrative plots may be no more—but of course also no less—than a variety of syntax which allows the verbal game—the dialogue, really—to go on.

To extend these implications further may be simply to encounter the commonplaces of artistic modernism, and these need to be tempered by a sense of the urgency of the narrative act, which may restitute reference and the "double logic" of narrative in other forms. But before turning to that consideration, I want to return to the specific issue of plot, to ask whether the story *Absalom, Absalom!* claims to tell ever gets told: whether the novel ever records the invention of a plot that is hermeneutically satisfying, and where our interpretive desire ought to rest its case. Here we must refer to a scene that ought to be a revelatory moment in both the story and its plot: a scene held in suspense nearly the length of the novel, and one that ought to offer key insight into Quentin's relationship to the narrative since it marks the moment at which the time of the narrators intersects with the time of the narrated—the moment at which it is revealed that one of the protagonists of the past drama lives on into the present of narration, offering the promise that the past can be recuperated within the present. This is of course Quentin's meeting with Henry Sutpen at Sutpen's Hundred in the fall of 1909, just before his departure for Harvard. What happens in this meeting?

> *And you are—?*
> *Henry Sutpen.*
> *And you have been here—?*
> *Four years.*
> *And you came home—?*
> *To die. Yes.*
> *To die?*
> *Yes. To die.*
> *And you have been here—?*
> *Four years.*
> *And you are—?*
> *Henry Sutpen.*

Does anything happen here? The passage reads as nearly a palindrome, virtually identical backward and forward, an unprogressive, reversible plot. It seems to constitute a kind of hollow structure, a concave mirror or black hole at the center of the narrative. It generates no light, no revelation. If we have been led to feel that we understand the events that precipitated the fall of the House of Sutpen, we may sense that we are still at a loss to understand the larger plot that should link the sons to the fathers, motivate not only the story from the past, but the present's relation to it.

We do know, however, that Quentin's narrating seems to impel him toward recollection and replay of the scene with Henry Sutpen, deferred to climactic position, disappointing in that it offers no revelation, yet evidently constitutive of compulsive narrative desire since the result of this scene for Quentin is "Nevermore of peace": an anxiety never to be mastered, a past come alive that never can be laid to rest. If we can understand in a general way how this "afterlife" of the Sutpen story creates an influx of energy which Quentin's narrative can never quite bind and discharge, can we say specifically why it is Henry Sutpen who emerges as the traumatic figure of Quentin's narrative desire?

We must face the question left hanging earlier: what is the motive of the narrating? One could address this question (and some critics have done so) by way of the intertextual relation between *Absalom, Absalom!* and *The Sound and the Fury,* calling upon Quentin's incestuous desire for his sister Candace to explain his fixation on the story of Henry, Judith, and Bon, equating Judith with Candace and Bon the seducer with Dalton Ames, thus assigning Henry and Quentin to the same tortured place in the triangle of desire. Yet *Absalom, Absalom!* doesn't even mention Quentin's having a sister, and in any case using the intertext to explain, rather than enrich and extend the novel, seems reductive and impoverishing. *Absalom, Absalom!* in fact offers no certain answer to the question of motivation. Yet I think it would also be a mistake simply to note the "arbitrariness" of the narrative and its undecidable relations of event and interpretation: so simplistic and sweeping a deconstructive gesture eludes the challenges the text poses to us. We should rather, I think, consider further how the text may suggest a remotivation of narrative through narration and the need for it.

As its title and its biblical intertext so clearly signal, *Absalom, Absalom!* addresses centrally the question of fathers and sons, perhaps the dominant thematic and structural concern and shaping force in the nineteenth-century novel, ultimately perhaps constituting a theme and a structure incorporate with the very nature of the novel as we know it. Circling about the problem of what Shreve calls "that one ambiguous eluded dark fatherhood," *Ab-*

salom, Absalom! raises the related issues of fraternity (Henry and Bon, Quentin and Shreve), paternity (including genealogy), and filiality (if I can know who my father is, will he consent to know me?). Eventually these issues may point to the problematic status of narrative meaning itself: meaning as a coherent patterning of relation and transmission, as the possibility of rule-governed selection and combination, as the sense-creating design of writing. Is coherent understanding, the explanatory narrative plotted from origin to endpoint, possible and transmissible? Do the sons inherit from the fathers, do they stand in structured and significant relation to an inheritance which informs the present? Can the past speak in a syntactically correct and comprehensible sentence?

Two threads of patterning, two elements of design, seem to be woven throughout the book. On the one hand there is incest, which according to Shreve (and Quentin does not contradict him) might be the perfect androgynous coupling, from which one would not have to uncouple: "maybe if there were sin too maybe you would not be permitted to escape, uncouple, return." Incest is that which overassimilates, denies difference, creates too much sameness. If, as Lévi-Strauss has claimed, it is the taboo on incest that creates the differentiated society, the attraction to incest raises the threat of the collapse of difference, loss of tension, and the stasis of desire extinguished in absolute satisfaction. On the other hand there is miscegenation, mixture of blood, the very trace of difference: that which overdifferentiates, creates too much difference, sets up a perpetual slippage of meaning where (as in the case of Charles Etienne Saint-Valery Bon brought before Justice Hamblett) one cannot find any points of fixity in the signifying chain. Incest thus would belong to the pole of metaphor, but as static, inactive metaphor, the same-as-same; whereas miscegenation would be a "wild," uncontrollable metonymy. The story of the House of Sutpen as told by the younger generation seems to be caught between these two figures, never able to interweave them in a coherent design. To give just one brief example, from the scene in Colonel Sutpen's camp in 1865, Quentin and Shreve narrate this exchange between Henry and Bon:

> —*You are my brother.*
> —*No I'm not. I'm the nigger that's going to sleep with your sister.*
> *Unless you stop me, Henry.*

Incest and miscegenation, sameness and difference, here as elsewhere in the narrative—including, notably, the working-out of Sutpen's design—fail to achieve a pattern of significant interweaving, and give instead a situation of paradox and impossibility: for instance, the nigger/brother conundrum that can be solved only by a pistol shot. Shreve at the end offers a parodic summing-up of this problem in design as it concerns the Sutpen "ledger" when he notes that it takes two Negroes to get rid of one Sutpen. "Which is all right, it's fine; it clears the whole ledger, you can tear all the pages out and burn them, except for one thing. . . . You've got one nigger left. One nigger Sutpen left. . . . You still hear him at night sometimes. Don't you?" The one left is, of course, Jim Bond, the idiot, the leftover who can be heard howling at night. The tale he would tell would be full of sound and fury, signifying nothing. He stands as a parodic version of Barthes's contention that the classical narrative offers at its end the implication of a residue of unexhausted meaning, a "pensivity" that remains to work in the reader.

The narrative ledger cannot be cleared by a neat calculation; the tale can never be plotted to the final, thorough, Dickensian accounting; and the *envoi* to the reader—the residual meaning embodied in Jim Bond—seems the very principle of nonsignificance. But of course this is not all that the text has to say about design and the making of patterns. Of the many metaphors of its own status and production presented by the text, all of which would bear consideration, I shall quote only Judith's extraordinary evocation of the loom, which she articulates when she comes to Quentin's grandmother, to ask her to keep the letter she received from Charles Bon during the war, a letter "without date or salutation or signature" which nonetheless constitutes a precious act of communication. It is an extended image, which moves from the letter to the entanglement of marionettes, which then modulates to the loom and the weaving of the rug, then moves on to another kind of text, the legend scratched on the tombstone, then back to the letter and the act of transmission of the letter:

> "and your grandmother saying, 'Me? You want me to keep it?' "
> " 'Yes,' Judith said, 'Or destroy it. As you like. Read it if you like or dont read it if you like. Because you make so little impression, you see. You get born and you try this and you dont know why only you keep on trying it and you are born at the same time with a lot of other people, all mixed up with them, like trying to, having to, move your arms and legs with strings only the same strings are hitched to all the other arms and legs and the others all trying and they dont know why either except that the strings are all in one another's way like five or six people all trying to make a rug on the same loom only each one wants to

weave his own pattern into the rug; and it cant matter, you know that, or the Ones that set up the loom would have arranged things a little better, and yet it must matter because you keep on trying or having to keep on trying and then all of a sudden it's all over and all you have left is a block of stone with scratches on it provided there was someone to remember to have the marble scratched and set up or had time to, and it rains on it and the sun shines on it and after a while they dont even re-member the name and what the scratches were trying to tell, and it doesn't matter. And so maybe if you could go to someone, the stranger the better, and give them something—a scrap of paper—something, anything, it not to mean anything in itself and them not even to read it or keep it, not even bother to throw it away or destroy it, at least it would be something just because it would have happened, be remembered even if only from pass-ing from one hand to another, one mind to another, and it would be at least a scratch, something, something that might make a mark on something that *was* once for the reason that it can die someday, while the block of stone cant be *is* because it never can become *was* because it cant ever die or perish.' "

If Judith's images suggest an ultimate pessimism about the status of texts—woven or graven or written—her insistence on passing on the fragile letter as an instance of something that possesses ontological gravity because it was written by a living hand, addressed from someone to someone, suggests that the process of sense-making retains a tenuous privilege of which its products are drained. Judith's statement concedes the evanescence or even the impossibility of the "referential" and "metalinguistic" functions of language (in Roman Jakobson's sense) while arguing the continuing pertinence of and need for the "phatic": the way we use language to test the communicative circuit, to confirm the conductive properties of the medium of words. She makes a claim neither for story nor for plot, but rather for narrating as, in Genette's terms, the narrative act productive of plot and story. This is not simply to state—in a modernist commonplace— that *Absalom, Absalom!* is a "poem about itself," but rather to contend that narrating is an urgent function in itself, that in the absence of pattern and structure, patterning and structuration remain necessary projects, dynamic intentions. Judith's struggle with the tenses of the verb "to be" suggests the whole problem of narrative as recovery of the past and makes us note how in the passing-on of Bon's letter of 1865 (whose very inscription—on the finest watermarked French notepaper taken from a gutted southern mansion, in stovepolish manufactured by the victorious Union and captured by the doomed Confederate raiders in the place of the food or ammunition they had hoped to find—is marked by the cosmic ironic laughter of History) the reader is linked not only to the reading but to the writing of "historical" documents, and how, as a belated reader of the document—following Judith herself, Quentin's grandmother, grandfather, father, and then Quentin himself—he is summoned to take his place in the activity of transmission, to join the ventriloquizd medium of history as fiction and fiction as history, perhaps finally to become, in a modification of Proust's phrase, the writer of himself.

The recovery of the past—which I take to be the aim of all narrative—may not succeed in *Absalom, Absalom!*, if by the recovery of the past we mean its integration within the present through a coherent plot fully predicated and understood as past. Yet the attempted recovery of the past makes known the continuing history of past desire as it persists in the present, shaping the project of telling. As the psychoanalyst Stanley Leavy has written, perhaps in too optimistic a tone, "All desire aims at the future, and this especially, because it is a desire for a revelatory knowledge to come, often first and naively experienced as the desire for the recovery of a buried memory, a lost trauma. To speak at all is to express the desire to be recognized and heard, whether the speech is in the form of a demand or not" (*The Psychoanalytic Dialogue*). The seemingly universal compulsion to narrate the past in *Absalom, Absalom!*, and to transmit its words, may speak both of an unmasterable past and of a dynamic narrative present dedicated to an interminable analysis of the past. Faulkner's present is a kind of tortured utopia of unending narrative dialogue informed by desire for a "revelatory knowledge." That knowledge never will come, yet that desire never will cease to activate the telling voices.

Quentin alludes to the tentative and dialogic quality of narrating in a parenthetic reference to General Compson's view of language: "language (that meager and fragile thread, Grandfather said, by which the little surface corners and edges of men's secret and solitary lives may be joined for an instant now and then before sinking back into the darkness where the spirit cried for the first time and was not heard and will cry for the last time and will not be heard then either)." This is certainly no triumphant apology for narrative; it makes the patternings of plot tentative indeed, ready to come unwoven as soon as they are stitched together. It is, perhaps, tentatively an apology for narrating, an enterprise apparently nostalgic, oriented toward the recovery of the past, yet really phatic in its vector, asking for hearing. I will here raise the question, to leave it unanswered, whether at the end of the novel Shreve has heard Quentin, whether his last question, "Why do you hate the South?" marks a failure of comprehension of all that has been told, or on the contrary too full an understanding of the desire animating the narrative act. And I will close by returning to the first agent of narration in the novel, Rosa Coldfield, to give her the last word, for it is she who speaks of *"the raging and incredulous recounting (which enables man to bear with living)."*

The "Joint" of Racism: Withholding the Black in *Absalom, Absalom!*

James A. Snead

In *Phaedrus,* Socrates praises the dialectician who can "survey scattered particulars . . . make a regular division and discover a characteristic mark of each class," and divide the classes "into species according to the natural formation, where the joint is." The "joint," in *Light in August, Absalom, Absalom!,* and *Go Down, Moses,* is where one tells one human class from another, and is the natural place of contrast where one may make a clean separation. But with color there are no clean separations; where does white end and black begin? The "joint," as such, is where the racial plot of the South holds together and threatens to fall apart. Since in racial discrimination "the characteristic mark of each class" is visual, and since all blood looks the same, both visual and "blood" distinctions destroy their own verifiability precisely at their "joint." The dialectician surveys "scattered particulars," finding skin color an apt visual signifier of difference. Subject and object take up conventionally fixed places: the viewers decide on a characteristic mark which becomes the static denotation of the viewed. Calling this classification "natural" hides its sources in fear, not nature, and attempts to underplay the arbitrariness of the mark.

Applying Socratic rhetorical division to social organization, it becomes clear that skin color is among the significations that have historically allowed human beings to be ranked, properly or improperly, within a hierarchy of oppositions. Frederic Jameson says that "the realm of separation, of fragmentation . . . exists, as Hegel would put it, not so much *in itself* as rather *for us,* as the basic logic and fundamental law of our daily life." Color is perhaps the most deceitful of all characteristic marks, because it seems self-evident, a division *in itself*—common sense says that everyone can agree upon the color of skin. Yet, compared to what all humans have in common (arms, legs, hair, blood, eyes), race is somewhat trivial, belonging to the category termed "deception" by Socrates himself: "When will there be more chance of deception—when the difference is large or small?" / "When the difference is small," Phaedrus correctly replies.

Sigmund Freud noticed that individuals decide upon small differences as the principle of individuation. In "The Taboo of Virginity," he notes that "every individual distinguishes himself from others by a 'taboo of personal isolation' . . . it is exactly the small differences, alongside an overall similarity, that were the basis for the feelings of strangeness and enmity between them." Freud's *Group Psychology and the Analysis of the Ego* suggests that human social relations might be constituted by what he calls "the narcissism of small differences":

> Closely related races keep one another at arm's length; the South German cannot endure the North German, the Englishman casts every kind of aspersion upon the Scot, the Spaniard despises the Portugese . . . greater differences . . . lead to an almost insuperable repugnance, such as the Gallic people feel for the German, the Aryan for the Semite, and the white races for the coloured.

But even these "greater differences" constitute an example of an anatomical fallacy that would systematically tie external to internal attributes.

Absalom, Absalom!, like its predecessor *Light in August*, systematically undercuts the outside–inside equation that the deceitful signs of race and gender are supposed to cement. Their incorrigibility—that Freud bemoans—comes from the fact that they share, in Paul de Man's words, the "property of language . . . the possibility of substituting binary polarities . . . without regard for the truth-value of these structures . . . this is precisely how Nietzsche also defines the rhetorical figure, the paradigm of all language." The crucial difference here is that southern segregationist discourse wishes to "freeze" as truth figures identifying skin color with value in coded signifier/signified pairs. For Nietzsche such rhetorical figures are unable to support a stable equivalence of exterior and interior—after all, the trope is exactly that which turns. As de Man suggests: "Rhetoric is a *text* in that it allows for two incompatible, mutually self-destructive points of view. . . . Considered as persuasion, rhetoric is performative, but when considered as a system of tropes, it deconstructs its own performance."

Faulkner's Charles Bon, like Joe Christmas, is a "black Caucasian" or "white Negro." Any conceptual configuration of strict racial division develops sprains in light or real oxymoronic figures such as these.

For racial identity is reciprocal. The black, as the white's "shadow"—borrowing Otto Rank's notion in *The Myth of the Birth of the Hero* of the "double" who figures the distance between ego-ideal and reality—evokes love (seen by the white as an offprint of himself) but also hate and fear (being a copy with an *Absalom, Absalom!* illustrates that barriers between the races are logically, psychologically, and sexually permeable). Freud suggests that in an "erotic" state in which "the boundary between ego and object threatens to melt away," we wish to reintegrate what has been separated. The loss of identity is a wish as well as a threat, belonging to "an earlier state of things"—the Urchaos of the womb ("the restoration of limitless narcissism"), a time when there were no social (or any other) divisions. As in every conceptual system, racial opposites rely on the other's signifying difference in order to mean anything at all. Society typically disregards this interlinkage, covering up the quantum of debt and guilt that each race must bear for the other. Charles Bon, in speaking to his innocent half brother Henry, exposes as false the independence of white women from black slave girls. He refers to "the slave girls and women upon whom that first caste [white virgin women] rested and to whom . . . it doubtless owed the very fact of its virginity." In short, the twin sexual taboos of the white southern male—against racial mixing, and against premarital sexual relations for the white woman—have become, in the face of *eros,* mutually exclusive. The "debt" that the virgin caste owes to black women despoiled also creates a residue of guilt in which the seeming polarities of white virgin and slave concubine inextricably commingle.

The vagueness of racial identity, in key moments, affects the ability even of whites to characterize themselves as anything at all. Miss Rosa, who on the surface represents white spinsterhood, is more mixed than she knows. She wears "eternal black" and sits in the darkness in a "black bonnet with jet sequins." She imagines herself as a child "standing motionless beside that door as though trying to make [herself] blend with the dark wood." On childhood trips to Sutpen's Hundred, her aunt "would order her to go and play with her nephew and niece," meaning Henry and Judith. Rosa's aunt does not mention Rosa's stepniece, Sutpen's black daughter, Clytie, and Rosa also ignores the family tie with Clytie. During her visits to Sutpen's mansion, Rosa "would not even play with the same objects which [Clytie] and Judith played with . . . the very objects [Clytie] had touched." Despite these hysterical precautions, Judith and Clytie have "even slept together, in the same room but with Judith in the bed and she on a pallet on the floor ostensibly." Rosa's "ostensibly" entails a further falsehood: in fact they are not lying separately side by side, but in the same bed: "I have heard how on more than one occasion Ellen has found them both on the pallet, and once in the bed together." Proximity becomes intimacy. Before long, Rosa has merged with her once tabooed stepniece, Clytie: Judith, Clytie, and Rosa lived "not as two white women and a negress, not as three negroes or three white, not even as three women, but merely as three creatures . . . with no distinction among the three of [them] of age or color. . . . It was as though [they] were one being, interchangeable and indiscriminate."

The most striking breakdown of racial division comes in the figure of Sutpen himself, about whom Faulkner cleverly leaves open the question of exact origins: "he didn't know just where his father had come from, whether from the country to which they returned or not, or even if his father knew, remembered, wanted to remember and find it again . . . he did not know within a year on either side just how old he was. So he knew neither where he had come from, nor where he was nor why." It soon becomes clear that Sutpen has produced in Clytie what Rosa calls the "Sutpen coffee-colored face," a black "replica of his own [face] which he had created and decreed to preside upon his absence." Yet like Charles Bon, Clytie, the replica, results from an intercourse of the races that, according to society's official view, may not exist. Given the overall valence of Sutpen in the novel as an absence that does not exist, it would seem that far from Clytie being a dark replica of his whiteness, Sutpen himself is the source of a certain censored blackness in the narrative. Sutpen introduces a kind of demonic "otherness" that seems to force open Jefferson's sureties of plot or language as if by fate or by accident. He is in fact the carrier of an origin-less blackness that clandestinely inserts its way into the presumably pure genealogies of southern whiteness.

Sutpen and blacks are twinned versions of what no system can either repress or signify for good. Sutpen's youth depicts the rejections that one typically finds in the lives of young blacks in white society. By the time Sutpen is older and arrives in Jefferson, he has almost completely merged with the "wild negroes," who "belonged to him body and soul": they are "distinguishable one from another by his beard and eyes alone . . . the bearded white man and the twenty black ones and all stark naked beneath the croaching and pervading mud." He fights "naked chest to chest" with the blacks, "both naked to the waist and gouging at one another's eyes as if they should not only have been the same color, but should have been

covered with fur too." Sutpen is a "public enemy" and a "runaway slave."
It becomes increasingly difficult, it seems, for any narrator to separate
Sutpen from the "wild negroes." Both habitually show their teeth, and
indeed in one case we see "his face exactly like the negro's save for the
teeth (this because of the beard, doubtless)." The teeth image is also the
last we see of Sutpen: Judith helps carry his corpse home, "quiet and bloody,
and his teeth still showing in the parted beard."

These mergings would be less noteworthy if they did not culminate
in Sutpen's merging with the one black whom he most wants to distance,
his son Charles Bon. Sutpen's characteristic "expression almost of smiling
where his teeth showed through the beard," his "something like smiling
inside his beard," and his final "looking at Henry with that expression
which might be called smiling" resonates in "Bon's teeth glinting for an
instant." The accidental repetition echoes a fundamental harmony. At one
point Judith says:

> You are born at the same time with a lot of other people, all
> mixed up with them, like trying to, having to, move your arms
> and legs with strings only the same strings are hitched to all the
> other arms and legs and the others . . . all trying to make a rug
> on the same loom only each one wants to weave his own pattern
> into the rug.

Her textual metaphor links society and Faulkner's narrative. Writing pretends an isolation of narrative strands that cannot last. Patterns intertwine.
Such an insight belongs to youth; Mark Twain's *Huckleberry Finn* has it;
we hear it in Mr. Compson's words: en route to college, Henry and Bon
were "only in surface manner of food and clothing and daily occupation
any different from the negro slaves who supported them." Sutpen and Bon
express, as the novel's key figures, tragic symmetries, both knocking at
closed doors and both rejected. Through the homology between Sutpen
and Bon, we can scan others: both marry without knowing their wives are
part black; both abandon their wives and sons; both are alternatively active
and passive; both are named and "nameless" shadows; both are present and
absent; both are futile avengers of prior affronts.

If Bon is one of "the white men," as he says, then the reversal of the
novel's standard reading is complete. It is incorrect to say that the white
Thomas Sutpen rejects his black son Charles Bon. Rather, Sutpen (like
Burch in *Light in August*) may be considerably "blacker" than we thought—
and perhaps most black where he wishes to be most white. In turning his
"black Caucasian" son away from his door, Sutpen has simply merged

with the same "monkey-dressed nigger" who first rebuffed him at a front door as a child. He, the father, has become black by turning back his putatively black son (we never learn whether in fact Bon has black blood). The climactic scene in the novel—the meeting between the aging Henry and Quentin—also figures a chiasmus structure, a turn of plot all the more compelling as it uses as its pivot exactly what has been made absent: the black. Faulkner's text illustrates that American caste and economic relations revolve around the black, the source of the paradoxes in Sutpen's story and American society's most volatile subject.

The main actors in the Sutpen story, by following logical steps forward from illogical premises, have created the sort of chaos they were hoping to dispel. They have reduced life to "jigsaw puzzle integers . . . inextricable, jumbled, and unrecognizable yet on the point of falling into a pattern." The energy of creating "a pattern" will always seem "on the point of" success, but instead "nothing happens." We are back to Judith's textual imagery of people "all trying to make a rug on the same loom only each one wants to weave his own pattern into the rug." Making solipsistic plans, as if this were not a world of interconnection, risks disastrous conclusions. Willed forgetting of others does not at all erase the other. Herbert Marcuse suggests that "the *return of the repressed* makes up the tabooed and subterranean history of civilization," and *Absalom, Absalom!* precisely illustrates such a return: the return of the black.

The absenting of society's repressed member becomes the place of greatest structural weakness in the social narrative that Shreve and Quentin, in the latter part of the novel, try to reconstruct, seam by seam. The omission of the central reference point, the black, disturbs as if by seismic influence the other coordinates that should be connected in normal narrative; everything makes sense when the effaced of society are brought back into the picture; without them, the picture "makes no sense." Judith's "loom" recalls an excerpt from Freud's "The Forgetting of Dreams":

> If the account of a dream seems at first difficult to understand,
> I ask the narrator to repeat it. This then rarely happens in the
> same words. But the places where he has altered the form of
> expression have marked themselves as the weak points of the
> dream disguise; they assist me like Hagen was assisted by the
> embroidered mark on Siegfried's cloak.

Freud's textual or narrative "hiatus" is indeed the Platonic joint where the dominant/subordinate divisions of the South stand ready to be slain. The repetition of the seemingly seamless text exposes the gap, the false assertion of autonomous pattern. The first telling repeats omissions; the second telling inserts truth as difference. The tale turns on the differences created by its omissions and later forced reinsertions of black presence.

Sutpen's "innocence" is a general innocence in white American society: innocent in the first place or ignorant about the violence that guarantees its identity; innocent secondly after the prior innocence is outgrown, because it believes that prior innocence can still be feigned. Sutpen, a victim of omissions, arrives repeatedly at a "withholding," a factual gap he cannot go beyond: "they deliberately withheld from me the one fact which I have reason to know they were aware would have caused me to decline the entire matter . . . this new fact rendered it impossible that this woman and child be incorporated in my design." Narrative "withholding" has been discussed frequently in the criticism of this novel (from Conrad Aiken's "deliberately withheld meaning" [1939] to Peter Brooks's "dilatory space" [1982]), without, however, having been seen in relationship to a general censorship and effacement of the black within the southern social narrative. In his perplexity, Sutpen recounts:

> " 'an arrangement [with his first wife's father] which I had en-
> tered in good faith, concealing nothing, while the other party
> or parties to it concealed from me the one very factor which
> would destroy the entire plan and design which I had been work-
> ing toward, concealed it so well that it was not until after the
> child was born that I discovered that this factor existed'—"

Sutpen's innocence here ("concealing nothing") is feigned: he has in fact concealed his entire design from his future father-in-law. We see above that Sutpen ends his own narrative with a hiatus. He never says explicitly that the withheld "factor" is race. His wife (Eulalia Bon) and child (Charles Bon) turn out to be black, but Sutpen withholds this fact from General Compson just as it has been withheld from him. The omission that interrupts Sutpen's narrative, then, the effacement of race, allows the narrative to continue. Sutpen's dark hiatus is his aporia as well—the shadow of blackness beyond which Henry, Shreve, and Quentin venture at their peril. The importance in psychoanalysis for such a moment of juncture merits these rare italics of Freud in "The Forgetting of Dreams": "*Whatever disturbs the continuation of the work is a resistance.*" Resistance or obstacles represent the reality which the patient's repetitions of false narratives continuously try to avoid.

The aporias here—figures of repeated confrontation and blockage— all involve the repressed blacks breaking out into whites' conscious awareness: the "nigger-servant," Clytie, or Bon. The dominant viewpoints from which we first encounter the Sutpen narrative (Rosa's and Mr. Compson's) require the expectation that its perspective point will be stable and unitary (the Cartesian "I" or "eye"). It is not what ophthalmology calls *stereoscopic vision,* which perceives depth by disparity or the slight *difference* between the images. In all cases, the repressed presence of the black, while adequate for the social text, causes interruptions of difference in the Sutpen narrative which prevent it from making sense. Sutpen, the "boy-symbol" has already been surprised by the silencing of racial division in the social text:

> It [racial segregation] had never once been mentioned by name,
> as when people talk about privation without mentioning the
> siege, about sickness without ever naming the epidemic.

The "unnameable," the absence, the "withheld" here is exactly the repressed black double that, by forcing differences into repeated narratives, returns to soil and spoil the point of view of white autonomy and dominance.

Although any story must select and withhold at times, *Absalom, Absalom!* reveals a social law through a narratological insight: society and the tale at first seem to function, but soon falter if one element is omitted consistently. Sutpen is like John Sartoris and Lucius McCaslin; he creates by sexual union black offprints or "replicas" of himself whose legitimacy he then tries to repress. The drive to suppress again and again a self-created double approximates the narrative's postponement of its promised final joinings: reconciliation or self-destruction of antagonists; sexual linkages between apparent racial opposites; the joining of hero and quest-object. A final merging is also fatal, because merging—as we also see in *The Sound and the Fury* or *As I Lay Dying*—betokens the death of identity.

Merging is in every sense "the end of narrative," and operates under the collapse of the appearance/reality or deception/truth pairs, wherein crossing-over to the suppressed term must compromise both the opposition and the story built upon it. Texts first correctly repeat an order, then challenge it through a dialectical routine, and finally the antagonisms of plot lead to a terminal resolution or dissolution of once strictly competitive sides. The relationship between what Faulkner calls "the general racial system in the South" and this narrative principle is the inverse: social logic encounters undifferentiated entities, divides them into "species," and then transmits that ranking as an exactly repeated narrative.

Summary and précis are habits of narrative that lead to the omission of blacks. One of the basic requirements for narrative must be the ability to tell which of the myriad details does and does not belong to the story.

The need to omit details gives to narrative the same license of exclusion that southern society enjoys with respect to its darker and poorer members. Withholding, then, becomes not merely the vagary of the individual consciousness, or the bad luck of the social climber, but rather a mechanism of all narrative, one not immune from being abused as social censorship. The expectation that a narrator will formulate the universal in the shape of a text results from the audience's (here Jefferson's) need for a consensus narrative in which it recognizes, as if in a flattering mirror, its own face. But the drive for self-recognition often means a refusal or inability to recognize others. Such a refusal, however, hides under the normal requirement for plot to withhold what does not belong.

Plot formation touches questions of history and time as well as of meaning. Creating a précis means reorganization, in a retrospective sense. But the reflective exercise of looking backwards reverses events, producing the illusion that history itself can, by acts of performative language, be revised. Sutpen thinks that "in the restoration of that ring to a living finger he had turned all time back twenty years and stopped it, froze it." In the timelessness of the psyche, history can seem a mere trope, reversible by raconteurial caprice. In general, the novel treats actual historical dates and Civil War events as secondary to the ability of the narrator, for reasons of evasion and censorship, to reorder the sequence and revise the significance of any given event.

Précis formation involves the censorship of memory (Freud's "waking redaction"). Variety reduced brings coherence; the précis systematically omits marginal figures. Sutpen suppresses the role of women in his design, failing to realize that he cannot achieve his dynasty without them. Moreover, the poor-white Wash—the laboring "nobody" of the South—finally must slay Sutpen, his erstwhile benefactor and friend. Reduction to epithet and précis fails because the repressed returns in the précis as *the idea of absence*. The "shadows" and "ghosts" of Rosa's narrative are the blacks that narrative precision (actually "*im*precision") has rendered invisible, and whose invisibility finally thwarts all efforts to understand the "why" of Sutpen's life: "it just does not explain" . . . "Yes, Judith, Bon, Henry, Sutpen: all of them. They are there, yet something is missing." The repetition of blacks' absence makes the exactly transmitted narrative incredible until Quentin and Shreve, as a last resort, restore the black, whose import as repeated absence everyone had overlooked all along.

But any such omission of the past quickly becomes a standard for the future. The normative tale becomes the social norm. There is more at stake here than simple narrative inaccuracy. Whatever it is said that people "usually do" will soon emerge as what people "must do" (the German *pflegen* and *Pflicht,* from the same root, have exactly these meanings). For many people, the step from what is done to what should be done, from the normal to the norm, is taken for granted. So the errors of omission that society hands down are probably inseparable from and simultaneous with a hoped-for social order. Yet racial separation destroys rather than creates order, and this may be the true moral of the Sutpen story. A shared paraphrase of events that excludes the black would be impossible without a consensus about reality that mirrors the unison participation of teller and listener. Perhaps for this reason it takes a Canadian, Shreve, to make the sense of the Sutpen story for which Quentin so desperately longs.

We have seen the importance of exact repetition and précis in narrative transmission. Now let us look at the epithets which facilitate the memo-rization of plot by reduction to simple marks. An epithetic plot, though exclusive, seems precise and well formed. The town's epithetic Sutpen narrative at the start of chapter 2 is instructive:

> It was the Chicksaw Indian agent with or through whom he dealt and so it was not until he waked the County Recorder that Saturday night with the deed, patent, to the land and the gold Spanish coin, that the town learned that he now owned a hundred square miles of some of the best virgin bottom land in the coun-try, though even that knowledge came too late because Sutpen himself was gone, where to again they did not know.

Sutpen's "hundred square miles of some of the best virgin bottom land in the country" later becomes "Sutpen's Hundred." Finally the Civil War reduces "Sutpen's Hundred" to "Sutpen's One," according to Miss Rosa. "Sutpen's Hundred" joins the "Chicksaw agent," the "Spanish coin," the "patent," the "roan horse," the "wild niggers," and the "French architect" as acceptable narrative abstractions of Sutpen's rise to power. Finally the name Sutpen is a reduction of what it concerns: Mr. Compson says "that nobody yet ever invented a name that somebody didn't own now or hadn't owned once" and Sutpen could be anyone—his story is "about something a man named Thomas Sutpen had experienced, which would still have been the same story if the man had had no name at all, if it had been told about any man or no man over whiskey at night." The name Sutpen is exactly a mnemonic epithet itself, a simplifying index for the town's vicarious experiences.

Since the name needs no specific tether of reference, it, too, may be exchanged, and the more so, the more acute the experience. Notice, for example, the erasure of names during the showdown between Bon and Henry:

> The one saying to Henry *I have waited long enough* and Henry saying to the other *Do you renounce then? Do you renounce?* and the other saying *I do not renounce* . . . the one calm and undeviating . . . the other remorseless with implacable and unalterable grief. . . . They faced one another on two gaunt horses, two men, young . . . the one with the tarnished braid of an officer, the other plain of cuff.

Under this summary supervision, Bon and Henry are "the one" and "the other." Likewise Quentin and Shreve become, mesmerized by the story's reducing effects, "as free now of flesh as the father who decreed and forbade, the son who denied and repudiated, the lover who acquiesced, the beloved who was not bereaved."

Perhaps the most clever instances of plot reduction are exactly like the one above, since the duplications of son, brother, sister, daughter are perfect opportunities for narrative duplicity. Miss Rosa's concise plot summary— "the son who widowed the daughter who had not yet been a bride"—tells us everything we need to know, but reveals nothing. A few pages later, she repeats it: "the daughter who was already the same as a widow without ever having been a bride . . . and the son who repudiated the very roof under which he had been born." By now, Miss Rosa has allowed the abstraction to replace the names; it is Quentin's problem to fill in the blanks. Even when Miss Rosa supplies certain names, she leaves out more important ones: "I saw Henry repudiate his home and birthright and then return and practically fling the bloody corpse of his sister's sweetheart at the hem of her wedding gown." If she had said "brother" instead of "sweetheart," we would already know of the censored incest. But this narration employs the clouding epithet "sweetheart."

Blacks are epithets ("niggers"), not persons. "Nigger" means unalterable abjectness rather than narrative terseness. Even the epithet nigger may be removed by parenthesis, so that we no longer even think of the reduction. Sutpen and Quentin's grandfather, for example, go with the "wild niggers" to hunt the "French architect" and we read that "the niggers had made camp and cooked supper and they (he and Grandfather) drank some of the whiskey and ate and then sat before the fire drinking some more of the whiskey and he telling it over." The parenthesis removes one of two possible grammatical ambiguities here, and does so in order to disconnect "the niggers" from "he and Grandfather" as possible referents of "they"—indeed it wishes to make the ambiguous pronoun "racially pure." The other personal pronoun, "*he* telling," remains equally ambiguous, but here there is no threat of interracial reference. More frequently though, blacks vanish without even being named by epithet. The town claims that Sutpen "lived out there, eight miles from any neighbor, in masculine solitude," but later we learn that two (black) women were indeed present in Sutpen's "masculine solitude": "Miss Rosa didn't tell you that two of the niggers in the wagon that day were women? . . . He brought the women deliberately; he probably chose them with the same care and shrewdness with which he chose the other livestock."

Quentin shares in the narrative erasure of blacks. At one point he describes Sutpen's: "two children—no, three," but soon after says "Yes, the two children, the son and the daughter." In fact, Sutpen has (at least) four children: one visibly black (Clytie); the other visibly white but called black (Bon); two others who are "pure" whites (Henry and Judith). Shreve surmises "So he just wanted a grandson," but in fact, Sutpen's designs were less temporally remote and racially neutral: he wanted a "pure white" son.

From the above discussion it should be obvious that the Sutpen story hides its truths in seemingly guileless forms—everyday figures of speech, innocuous habits of expression, sudden forgettings. For instance, the town speculates on the relationship between Bon and Henry: "They would be seen together in the carriage in town now . . . which certainly would not have been the case if the quarrel had been between Bon and the father, and probably not the case if the trouble had been between Henry and his father." Already the difference between "the" and "his" father conceals the fact that the father in both cases is the same person. When Mr. Compson says "that Bon's intention . . . was apparently to make his (Henry's) sister a sort of junior partner in a harem," his bracket removes the possibility that Judith is Bon's sister, by clarifying "his" as "Henry's." Such clarification however increases rather than decreases what Socrates calls the deception of reductive classification.

Even if the epithet successfully reduces, omits, and repeats the social plot, still "it just does not explain" because logical coherence has given way to relations of dominance and submission. Following a traditional sequence of actions from cause to effect is impossible in *Absalom, Absalom!*, but this fact should hardly be taken as a criticism of Faulkner's literary skill. For his narrators interchange and rearrange epithets at will without harming the essential process of the story, which is finally neither to relay historical facts and dates, nor to describe a linear sequence of logically coherent events, but rather to establish a narrational regimen that allows a particular story to be told repeatedly in a certain way.

For *Absalom, Absalom!* is not primarily either about Sutpen or about Harvard or Jefferson in 1909. The narrator of the novel "sets" us in these contexts, but the individual narrators hardly mention the physical setting in which they find themselves relating their stories. Quentin, Rosa, Shreve, and Mr. Compson engage their listeners, but ignore their environments. Indeed, the Sutpen story might "be told about any man or no man," because the telling of the story is really a sort of induction rite, testing the novitiate's ability to learn and tactfully transmit the secret sleight of hand upon which racial classifications are based. The story both hides and exposes "two hundred years of oppression and exploitation [of the black]" as well as the continued exploitation of those victims' children and grandchildren, refusing to speak of things that are plain to see. As an apprentice, the listener should never betray the mechanics of such racial legerdemain. For the parable says to its white southern auditors, "ignore that the black is deeply implicated in all you do, and ignore that the story makes no sense when you ignore the black." The initiate and listener both escape despair at this message by transmitting it automatically without questioning or even understanding its true injunction. Shreve has punctured this smooth fabric, saying that "the story makes sense if you restore the black; it fails otherwise," but even by mentioning the black, he has already failed the story. And Quentin has failed even more grandly, because he (and his southern informants) have failed to impose through their narrations the South's influential magic upon the shrewd Canadian listener.

Chronology

1897	Born William Cuthbert Falkner, in New Albany, Mississippi, on September 25; first child of Murry Falkner, then a railroad executive, and Maud Butler.
1914	Leaves school after long history as a poor student.
1916–17	Lives on fringe of student community at the University of Mississippi.
1918	Tries to enlist in U.S. armed forces, but is refused. Works in New Haven, Connecticut, for Winchester Gun factory. Changes spelling of name from "Falkner" to "Faulkner." Enlists in Canadian Air Force, but war ends while he is still in training.
1919	Returns to Oxford and enters the University of Mississippi. Writes poems that will be included in *The Marble Faun*.
1920	Leaves the university, but remains in Oxford.
1921	After spending autumn in New York City, returns to Oxford to work as postmaster.
1924	Resigns postmastership; *The Marble Faun*.
1925–26	New Orleans period, frequently in circle surrounding Sherwood Anderson. Writes *Soldiers' Pay* and *Mosquitoes;* travels to Europe and resides in Paris; returns to Oxford.
1927	Writes *Flags in the Dust,* which is rejected.
1928	Writes *The Sound and the Fury*.
1929	*Sartoris* (curtailed version of *Flags in the Dust*) published. Marriage of Faulkner and Estelle Franklin on June 20. Finishes *Sanctuary;* publishes *The Sound and the Fury;* begins *As I Lay Dying*.
1930	Finishes and publishes *As I Lay Dying;* revises *Sanctuary*.
1931	Daughter Alabama is born in January and dies the same month. *Sanctuary* published; begins *Light in August*.

143

1932   Finishes *Light in August,* which is published after his father's death; begins first Hollywood screenwriting period.

1933   *A Green Bough;* daughter Jill born.

1934   *Doctor Martino and Other Stories.*

1935   *Pylon.*

1936   *Absalom, Absalom!*

1938   *The Unvanquished.*

1939   *The Wild Palms.*

1940   *The Hamlet.*

1942   *Go Down, Moses.*

1946   *The Portable Faulkner.*

1948   *Intruder in the Dust.*

1949   *Knight's Gambit.*

1950   *Collected Stories;* Nobel Prize in literature.

1951   *Requiem for a Nun.*

1954   *A Fable.* First assignment for State Department.

1955   Goes to Japan for State Department.

1957   *The Town.*

1959   *The Mansion.*

1960   Faulkner's mother dies.

1962   *The Reivers.* Faulkner dies in Byhalia, Mississippi, on July 6, from coronary occlusion.

Contributors

HAROLD BLOOM, Sterling Professor of the Humanities at Yale University, is the author of *The Anxiety of Influence, Poetry and Repression* and many other volumes of literary criticism. His forthcoming study, *Freud: Transference and Authority*, attempts a full-scale reading of all of Freud's major writings. A MacArthur Prize Fellow, he is general editor of five series of literary criticism published by Chelsea House. During 1987–88, he was appointed Charles Eliot Norton Professor of Poetry at Harvard University.

JOHN T. IRWIN is Chairman of the Writing Seminars at The Johns Hopkins University. His works include *American Hieroglyphics* and *The Heisenberg Variations*, a volume of poems published under the name of John Bricuth.

GARY LEE STONUM teaches at Case Western Reserve University and is the author of *Faulkner's Career: An Internal Literary History*.

CAROLYN PORTER is Associate Professor at the University of California, Berkeley, and the author of *Seeing and Being: The Plight of the Participant Observer in Emerson, James, Adams, and Faulkner*.

DAVID MINTER is Dean of Emory College and Professor of English at Emory University. His works include *The Interpreted Design* and *William Faulkner*.

ERIC J. SUNDQUIST teaches at the University of California, Berkeley. He has written *Home as Found: Authority and Genealogy in Nineteenth-Century American Literature* and edited *American Realism: New Essays*.

PETER BROOKS is Tripp Professor of the Humanities at Yale University. He is the author of *The Novel of Worldliness, The Melodramatic Imagination*, and *Reading for the Plot*.

JAMES A. SNEAD, Assistant Professor of English and Comparative Literature at Yale University, is the author of *Figures of Division: William Faulkner's Major Novels*.

Bibliography

Bleikasten, André. "Fathers in Faulkner." In *The Fictional Father: Lacanian Readings of the Text,* edited by Robert Con Davis, 115–46. Amherst: University of Massachusetts Press, 1981.

Bloom, Harold, ed. *Modern Critical Views: William Faulkner.* New York: Chelsea House, 1986.

Blotner, Joseph Leo. *Faulkner, A Biography.* New York: Random House, 1974.

———. "The Falkners and the Fictional Families." *The Georgia Review* 30 (1976): 572–92.

Brodhead, Richard H., ed. *Faulkner: New Perspectives.* Englewood Cliffs, N.J.: Prentice-Hall, 1983.

Brooks, Cleanth. "The Narrative Structure of *Absalom, Absalom!*" In *William Faulkner: Toward Yoknapatawpha and Beyond,* 301–28. New Haven: Yale University Press, 1978.

———. *William Faulkner: First Encounters.* New Haven: Yale University Press, 1983.

———. *The Yoknapatawpha Country.* New Haven: Yale University Press, 1963.

Brooks, Peter. *Reading for the Plot: Design and Intention in Narrative.* New York: Knopf, 1984.

Brown, Calvin. *A Glossary of Faulkner's South.* New Haven: Yale University Press, 1976.

Carey, Glenn O., ed. *Faulkner: The Unappeased Imagination: A Collection of Critical Essays.* Troy, N.Y.: Whitston, 1980.

Cox, Leland H., ed. *William Faulkner: Biographical and Reference Guide.* Detroit: Gale Research Company, 1982.

Doody, Terrence. *Confession and Community in the Novel.* Baton Rouge: Louisiana State University Press, 1980.

Faulkner Studies, 1980–.

Faulkner, William. *Faulkner in the University: Class Conferences at the University of Virginia, 1957–1959.* Edited by Joseph Blotner and Frederick L. Gwynn. New York: Vintage, 1966.

———. *Selected Letters of William Faulkner.* Edited by Joseph Blotner. New York: Random House, 1978.

———. *William Faulkner: Essays, Speeches, Public Letters.* Edited by James B. Meriwether. New York: Random House, 1965.

Goldman, Arnold, ed. *Twentieth Century Interpretations of* Absalom, Absalom! Englewood Cliffs, N.J.: Prentice-Hall, 1971.

Gray, Richard J. *The Literature of Memory: Modern Writers of the American South.* Baltimore: Johns Hopkins University Press, 1976.

Guetti, James. *The Limits of Metaphor: A Study of Melville, Conrad, and Faulkner.* Ithaca: Cornell University Press, 1967.

Harrington, Evans, and Ann J. Abadie, eds. *The South and Faulkner's Yoknapatawpha: The Actual and the Apocryphal.* Jackson: University Press of Mississippi, 1977.

Howe, Irving. *William Faulkner, A Critical Study.* New York: Vintage, 1962. Chicago: University of Chicago Press, 1975.

Irwin, John T. *Doubling and Incest / Repetition and Revenge: A Speculative Reading of Faulkner.* Baltimore: Johns Hopkins University Press, 1975.

Jehlen, Myra. *Class and Character in Faulkner's South.* New York: Columbia University Press, 1976.

Kartiganer, Donald M. *The Fragile Thread: The Meaning of Form in Faulkner's Novels.* Amherst: University of Massachusetts Press, 1979.

Kinney, Arthur F. *Faulkner's Narrative Poetics. Style as Vision.* Amherst: University of Massachusetts Press, 1978.

———. "Form and Function in *Absalom, Absalom!*" *The Southern Review* 14 (1978): 677–961.

Krause, David. "Reading Shreve's Letters and Faulkner's *Absalom, Absalom!*" *Studies in American Fiction* 11 (1983): 153–69.

Levin, Lynn G. "The Four Narrative Perspectives of *Absalom, Absalom!*" *PMLA* 85 (1970): 35–47.

Matlack, James H. "The Voices of Time: Narrative Structure in *Absalom, Absalom!*" *The Southern Review* 15 (1979): 333–54.

Matthews, John T. *The Play of Faulkner's Language.* Ithaca: Cornell University Press, 1982.

Meriwether, James B. *The Literary Career of William Faulkner.* Princeton: Princeton University Press, 1961.

Meriwether, James B., and Michael Millgate, eds. *Lion in the Garden: Interviews with William Faulkner, 1926–1962.* New York: Random House, 1968.

Miller, J. Hillis. "The Two Relativisms: Point of View and Indeterminacy in the Novel *Absalom, Absalom!*" In *Relativism in the Arts,* edited by Betty Jean Craige, 148–70. Athens: University of Georgia Press, 1983.

Millgate, Michael. *The Achievement of William Faulkner.* New York: Random House, 1966.

Minnesota Review 21 (1981). Special Faulkner issue.

Minter, David. *William Faulkner: His Life and Work.* Baltimore: Johns Hopkins University Press, 1980.

Muhlenfeld, Elisabeth. "We Have Waited Long Enough: Judith Sutpen and Charles Bon." *The Southern Review* 14 (1978): 66–80.

Parker, Robert Dale. *Faulkner and the Novelistic Imagination.* Urbana: University of Illinois Press, 1985.

Parr, Susan Resneck. "The Fourteenth Image of the Blackbird: Another Look at Truth in *Absalom, Absalom!*" *Arizona Quarterly* 35 (Summer 1979): 153–64.

Pitavy, François. "The Gothicism of *Absalom, Absalom!*: Rosa Coldfield Revisited." In *"A Cosmos of My Own": Faulkner and Yoknapatawpha, 1980,* edited by Doreen Fowler and Ann J. Abadie, 199–226. Jackson: University Press of Mississippi, 1981.

Poirier, Richard. " 'Strange Gods' in Jefferson, Mississippi: Analysis of *Absalom, Absalom!*" In *William Faulkner: Two Decades of Criticism,* edited by Frederick J. Hoffman and Olga W. Vickery, 217–43. East Lansing: Michigan State University Press, 1951.

Porter, Carolyn. *Seeing and Being: The Plight of the Participant Observer in Emerson, James, Adams, and Faulkner.* Middletown, Conn.: Wesleyan University Press, 1981.

Rio-Jelliffe, R. "*Absalom, Absalom!* as Self-Reflexive Novel." *Journal of Narrative Technique* 11, no. 2 (1981): 75–90.

Rose, Maxine. "Echoes of the King James Bible in the Prose Style of *Absalom, Absalom!*" *Arizona Quarterly* 37, no. 2 (1981): 37–48.

Ross, Stephen M. "The Evocation of Voice in *Absalom, Absalom!*" *Essays in Literature* 8 (1981): 135–49.

Ruppersburg, Hugh M. *Voice and Eye in Faulkner's Fiction.* Athens: University of Georgia Press, 1983.

Schoenberg, Estella. *Old Tales and Talking: Quentin Compson in William Faulkner's* Absalom, Absalom! *and Related Works.* Jackson: University Press of Mississippi, 1977.

Slatoff, Walter J. *Quest for Failure: A Study of William Faulkner.* Ithaca: Cornell University Press, 1960.

Stonum, Gary Lee. *Faulkner's Career: An Internal Literary History.* Ithaca: Cornell University Press, 1979.

Sundquist, Eric J. *Faulkner: The House Divided.* Baltimore: Johns Hopkins University Press, 1983.

Vickery, Olga. *The Novels of William Faulkner.* Baton Rouge: Louisiana State University Press, 1964.

Warren, Robert Penn, ed. *Faulkner: A Collection of Critical Essays.* Englewood Cliffs, N.J.: Prentice-Hall, 1966.

Watkins, Evan. *The Critical Act: Criticism and Community.* New Haven: Yale University Press, 1978.

———. "The Fiction of Interpretation: Faulkner's *Absalom, Absalom!*" In *The Critical Act: Criticism and Community.* New Haven: Yale University Press, 1978.

Wittenberg, Judith Bryant. *Faulkner: The Transfiguration of Biography.* Lincoln: University of Nebraska Press, 1979.

Wyatt, David M. *Prodigal Sons: A Study in Authorship and Authority.* Baltimore: Johns Hopkins University Press, 1979.

Young, Thomas Daniel. "Narration as Creative Act: The Role of Quentin Compson in *Absalom, Absalom!*" In *Faulkner, Modernis, and Film,* edited by Evans Harrington and Ann J. Abadie. Jackson: University Press of Mississippi, 1979.

Acknowledgments

"Doubling and Incest / Repetition and Revenge" by John T. Irwin from *Doubling and Incest / Repetition and Revenge: A Speculative Reading of Faulkner* by John T. Irwin, © 1975 by the Johns Hopkins University Press, Baltimore/London. Reprinted by permission of the Johns Hopkins University Press.

"The Fate of Design" by Gary Lee Stonum from *Faulkner's Career: An Internal Literary History* by Gary Lee Stonum, © 1979 by Cornell University. Reprinted by permission of Cornell University Press.

"William Faulkner: Innocence Historicized" (originally entitled "Faulkner's America") by Carolyn Porter from *Seeing and Being: The Plight of the Participant Observer in Emerson, James, Adams, and Faulkner* by Carolyn Porter, © 1981 by Carolyn Porter. Reprinted by permission of Wesleyan University Press.

"Family, Region, and Myth in Faulkner's Fiction" by David Minter from *Faulkner and the Southern Renaissance: Faulkner and Yoknapatawpha, 1981,* edited by Doreen Fowler and Ann J. Abadie, © 1982 by the University Press of Mississippi. Reprinted by permission of the University Press of Mississippi.

"*Absalom, Absalom!* and the House Divided" by Eric J. Sundquist from *Faulkner: The House Divided* by Eric J. Sundquist, © 1983 by the Johns Hopkins University Press, Baltimore/London. Reprinted by permission of the Johns Hopkins University Press.

"Incredulous Narration: *Absalom, Absalom!*" by Peter Brooks from *Reading for the Plot: Design and Intention in Narrative* by Peter Brooks, © 1984 by Peter Brooks. Reprinted by permission of Alfred A. Knopf, Inc., and the Clarendon Press.

"The 'Joint' of Racism: Withholding the Black in *Absalom, Absalom!*" by James A. Snead, © 1987 by James A. Snead. Published for the first time in this volume. Printed by permission. A slightly different form of this article appeared in *Figures of Division: William Faulkner's Major Novels* (New York: Methuen, 1986), © 1986 by James A. Snead.

Index

153